St. Louis Cardinals
Past & Present

Doug Feldmann

MVP BOOKS

First published in 2009 by MVP Books, an imprint of MBI Publishing and the Quayside Publishing Group, 400 First Avenue N, Suite 300, Minneapolis, MN 55401 USA

Text copyright © 2009 by Doug Feldmann

All rights reserved. With the exception of quoting brief passages for the purposes of review, no part of this publication may be reproduced without prior written permission from the Publisher.

The information in this book is true and complete to the best of our knowledge. All recommendations are made without any guarantee on the part of the author or Publisher, who also disclaim any liability incurred in connection with the use of this data or specific details.

We recognize, further, that some words, model names, and designations mentioned herein are the property of the trademark holder. We use them for identification purposes only. This is not an official publication.

MVP Books are also available at discounts in bulk quantity for industrial or sales-promotional use. For details write to Special Sales Manager at Quayside Publishing, 400 First Avenue North, Suite 300, Minneapolis, MN 55401 USA.

Library of Congress Cataloging-in-Publication Data

Feldmann, Doug, 1970–
 St. Louis Cardinals past & present / Doug Feldmann.—1st ed.
  p. cm.
 ISBN 978-0-7603-3528-4 (hb w/ jkt)
 1. St. Louis Cardinals (Baseball team)—History. I. Title.
 GV875.S3F465 2009
 796.357'640977866—dc22
                                    2008038257

Editor: Josh Leventhal
Designer: Jennie Tischler

Printed in China

On the front cover: (top left) Stan Musial, circa 1955; (top right) Chris Carpenter, 2007; (bottom) Busch Stadium III, 2007.
On the title page: (main) Busch Stadium III at night, 2007; (inset) Sportsman's Park, 1944 World Series.
On the back cover: (top left) St. Louis Cardinals, 1930; (top right) St. Louis Cardinals, 2008; (bottom left) Rogers Hornsby, 1926; (bottom right) Albert Pujols, 2003.

Contents

Acknowledgments	7	Relievers	90
Cardinals Yesterday, Cardinals Today	8	The Name Game	94
The Great Teams and the Dynasties	10	Homegrown Heroes	98
The World Series	14	Bad Boys	100
Gaffes and Controversies	21	Hard-Luck Players	104
The Rivalries	24	Superstitions and Musical Beats	108
The Owners	28	Uniforms and Equipment	110
The General Managers	32	The Ballparks	114
Breaking the Race Barrier	36	The Playing Field and Outfield Dimensions	120
The Managers	38	The Dugouts, Clubhouses, and Bullpens	122
Catchers	44	The Scoreboards and Billboards	124
First Basemen	50	The Fans	126
Hit Men	56	The Cardinals and the All-Star Game	130
Second Basemen	60	Voices of the Cardinals	132
Shortstops	64	Spring Training	136
Third Basemen	68	Down on the Farm	138
Outfielders	72		
The Jackrabbits	78	Bibliography and Resources	140
The Home Run Kings	82	Index	141
Starting Pitchers	84	About the Author	144

Photo and Illustration Credits

We wish to acknowledge the following for providing the illustrations included in the book. Every effort has been made to locate the copyright holders for materials used, and we apologize for any oversights. Unless otherwise noted, all other images are from the publisher's collection. Individual photographers and collections are listed for photographs when known.

AP/Wide World Photos: p. 3, 12 top and bottom; 13 left; 13 right (Amy Sancetta); 16 top; 17 top; 18 bottom; 19 top; 20 top (Amy Sancetta); 24 left; 25 top; 26 top (Edward Kitch); 26 bottom (Chris Carlson); 27 bottom left (Beth A. Keiser); 27 right (Tom Gannam); 29 top and bottom; 30 top and bottom; 32 left and right; 33 top; 34 bottom (James A. Finley); 37 (Lynne Sladky); 39 left and right; 40 left and right; 41 top; 41 bottom left (Paul Cannon); 42 top; 43 left (Rusty Kennedy); 46; 47 top and bottom (Focus On Sport); 48 top (Focus On Sport); 52 bottom (Gene Smith); 62 left; 65 top; 67 left (Tom Gannam); 67 right (Jeff Roberson); 68 right; 69 top; 73 top and bottom (Preston Stroup); 74 left and right; 75 bottom (Roberto Borea); 76 bottom (Kyle Ericson); 77 (Morry Gash); 79 top and bottom; 82 right; 83 top; 83 bottom left (John Gaps III); 86 top; 88 top; 91 top right and bottom; 92; 95 bottom; 97 top (James A. Finley); 98 left; 104; 105 top (Tom Gannam); 105 bottom (James A. Finley); 106 top (Jeffrey Phelps); 107 left and right (Tom Gannam); 111 bottom; 118 (James A. Finley); 119 top (Tom Gannam); 121 top right (Mary Butkus); 122 bottom right; 127 top; 128 top (James A. Finley); 130; 131 bottom; 132 left and right; 133 top (Tom Gannam); 134 top (Leon Algee); 134 bottom (Tom Gannam); 135 top; 137 bottom (Rob Carr); 138 left (John Flavell); 138 right (Beau Rogers); 139 top (John S. Stewart); 139 bottom (John L. Focht).

George Brace Collection: p. 45 bottom; 85 bottom; 95 top right; 96 left; 108.

Getty Images: p. 7 (Ronald C. Modra/Sports Imagery); 19 bottom (Focus on Sport); 22 (Focus on Sport); 23 top and bottom right (Focus on Sport); 23 bottom left (Ronald C. Modra/Sports Imagery); 25 bottom (Focus on Sport); 27 top left (Rogers Photo Archive); 31 top (Focus on Sport); 31 bottom (Rich Pilling/MLB Photos); 34 top (Ronald C. Modra/Sports Imagery); 35 (Rich Pilling/MLB Photos); 36 top (Art Rickerby/Diamond Images); 37 top (Louis Requena/MLB Photos); 41 bottom right (Focus on Sport); 42 bottom (Focus on Sport); 48 bottom (Otto Greule Jr.); 63 top (MLB Photos); 64 right (Bruce Bennett Studios); 65 bottom (Focus on Sport); 66 top (Ronald C. Modra/Sports Imagery); 66 bottom (Focus on Sport); 68 left (FPG); 69 bottom (Focus on Sport); 70 right (Focus on Sport); 75 top (Focus on Sport); 76 top (Focus on Sport); 78 (Bruce Bennett Studios); 80 (Ronald C. Modra/Sports Imagery); 81 top (Otto Greule Jr.); 81 bottom (Stephen Dunn/Allsport); 87 top and bottom (Focus on Sport); 88 bottom left (Ronald C. Modra/Sports Imagery); 93 left (Focus on Sport); 98 right (Michael Zagaris/Time Life Pictures); 101 top (FPG); 101 bottom (Hulton Archive); 102 (Ronald C. Modra/Sports Imagery); 103 (Focus on Sport); 109 bottom (Ezra Shaw); 112 (Louis Requena/MLB Photos); 113 top (Focus on Sport); 113 bottom left (Bruce Bennett Studios); 116 bottom right (Dan Donovan/MLB Photos); 120 (MLB Photos); 122 bottom left (Ronald C. Modra/Sports Imagery); 123 top (Ronald C. Modra/Sports Imagery); 123 bottom (Elsa); 124 (Dilip Vishwanat); 126 bottom (APA); 127 bottom (Rob Tringali/Sportschrome); 128 bottom (Rich Pilling/MLB Photos); 129 top and bottom (Elsa); 131 top (John Vawter Collection), front cover top left.

Library of Congress, Prints and Photographs Division: p. 8 bottom; 9 top left; 11 top left; 28 top left, bottom left, and bottom right; 38 top (Bain Collection); 38 bottom; 44 left; 44 right (Bain Collection); 50 left and right; 56; 60 left and right; 64 left; 72 left; 84 left; 84 right (Bain Collection); 110 left; 110 right (Bain Collection).

National Baseball Hall of Fame Library, Cooperstown, N.Y.: p. 9 top right, middle right, bottom left; 11 bottom; 15 bottom; 21; 53 left and right; 57 left and right; 58 left; 62 right; 90; 96 right; 114 bottom; 115 bottom; 121 top left; 136 top.

Scott Rovak: p. 2, 9 bottom right; 20 bottom; 43 right; 49 left and right; 54 bottom; 55; 59; 63 bottom left and bottom right; 71 top and bottom; 83 bottom right; 89 left and right; 93 right; 99; 106 bottom; 113 bottom right; 116 top left; 117 top and bottom; 133 bottom; 137 top right, front cover top right.

Shutterstock: p. 119 bottom; 121 bottom; 125 bottom.

Transcendental Graphics/The Rucker Archive: p. 8 top; 9 middle left; 10; 14 left and right; 15 top; 16 bottom; 17 bottom; 18 top; 33 bottom; 36 bottom; 45 top; 51 left and right; 58 right; 61 top and bottom; 70 left; 72 right; 82 left; 85 top; 86 bottom; 91 top left; 94; 97 bottom; 100; 109 top; 111 top; 114 top; 126 top; 136 bottom.

Acknowledgments

The author would like to thank the following individuals and organizations who provided photographs included herein: Scott Rovak, Mary Brace of the George Brace Collection, Mark Rucker of Transcendental Graphics, John Horne at the National Baseball Hall of Fame, Deborah Cribbs and the St. Louis Mercantile Library at the University of Missouri–St. Louis, the Associated Press, Getty Images, and the United States Library of Congress.

A special note of thanks to my editor at MVP Books, Josh Leventhal, whose assistance and encouragement throughout the process of writing this book was invaluable.

Ozzie Smith making his patented dramatic entrance, 1985 World Series

Cardinals Yesterday, Cardinals Today

St. Louis is often referred to as the best baseball city in America, and the Cardinals are certainly the crown jewel of that distinction. Entering the professional ranks as the Brown Stockings in the American Association in 1882, the franchise switched to the name of Browns the following year, the Perfectos in 1899, and finally the Cardinals in 1900. (This was not the first or the last St. Louis team to embrace the Browns or Brown Stockings moniker. The unrelated St. Louis club that was an inaugural member of the National League in 1876 was known as the Brown Stockings during its two years of existence. Also unrelated, the commonly known American League team called the Browns came into existence in 1902.)

As a baseball empire in the first half of the twentieth century, the expanse of the Cardinals' popularity was as vast as any had seen; for up until the expansion of Major League Baseball in the 1960s, St. Louis was the western-most and southern-most major league city. As a result, the Cardinals developed a following of fans wide and deep through the heartland.

While the uniforms, players, and even ballparks changed through the decades, at least one feature of the Cardinals has remained constant: their steady success in the standings. Their 10 world championships—accumulated in six different decades—are tops among all National League franchises, and their 17 pennants are the most by any National League team in one location, trailing only the combined pennant totals of the Brooklyn–Los Angeles Dodgers (21) and the New York–San Francisco Giants (20). With Hall of Famers from Rogers Hornsby to Osborne "Ozzie" Smith, Jay "Dizzy" Dean to Bob Gibson, Stan "The Man" Musial to, perhaps, Albert Pujols, the Cardinals have featured an all-star cast for more than a century.

St. Louis Browns, 1883

St. Louis Cardinals, 1909

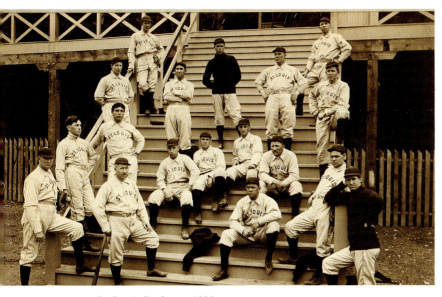

St. Louis Perfectos, 1899

St. Louis Cardinals, 1930

St. Louis Cardinals, 1942

St. Louis Cardinals, 1967

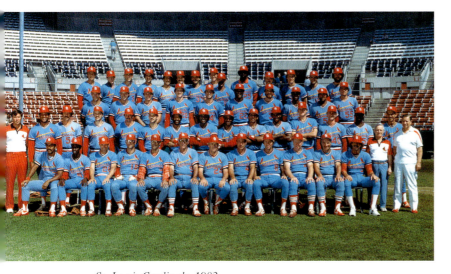

St. Louis Cardinals, 1982

St. Louis Cardinals, 2008

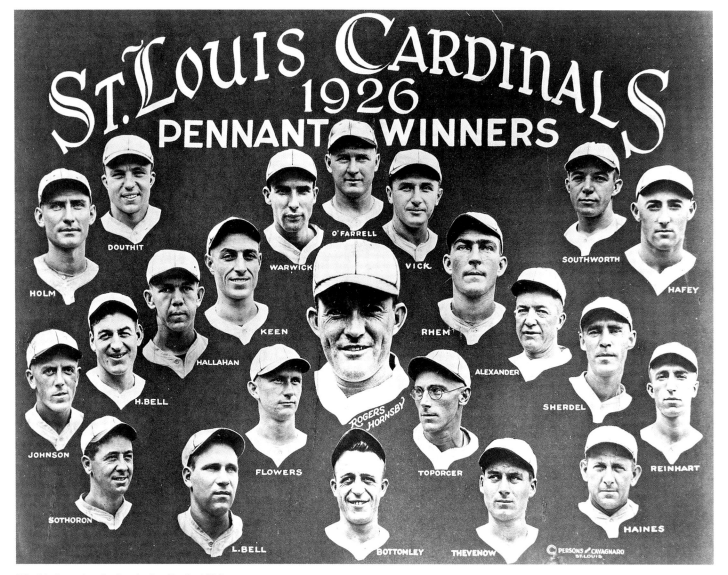

World champion St. Louis Cardinals, 1926

The Great Teams and the Dynasties

St. Louis' winning ways extend back to the franchise's first decade, when Charles Comiskey's Browns won four consecutive American Association crowns (1885–1888). The team posted three more winning seasons, but after St. Louis switched to the National League in 1892, the team entered a prolonged rut.

Led by Hall of Famers Rogers Hornsby, Jim Bottomley, Jesse Haines, and Pete Alexander, the Cardinals returned to the top in the 1920s, winning their first National League pennant in 1926. Although some of the characters changed—for example, Hornsby was exchanged for another Hall of Fame second baseman, Frankie Frisch, in 1927—the Cardinals won a total of five pennants in nine seasons.

The storied "Gas House Gang" was a perennial force in the Senior Circuit during the early 1930s, posting the franchise's first 100-win season in 1931 (101–53). Later in the decade, pitcher Dizzy Dean took center stage under player-manager Frankie Frisch, while Ripper Collins and Joe Medwick provided muscle at the plate, and Johnny "Pepper" Martin provided lots of spark.

The great Cardinals teams of the 1930s transitioned nearly seamlessly to a new roster of stars in the 1940s. Aging Gas House Gang heroes like Martin, the Dean brothers, and Medwick gave way to a new generation of favorites in Stan Musial, Enos Slaughter, and Albert "Red" Schoendienst, while regulars such as Johnny Mize and Mickey Owen had the pleasure of playing with both esteemed collections. After a second-place finish in 1941, the team won three straight pennants in 1942, 1943, and 1944 and added a fourth in 1946, winning the World Series each of these years except 1943. The 1942 outfit is considered one of the greatest in club history—its .688 winning percentage (106–48) stands as the franchise's best in the modern era.

"The Famous World Beaters," St. Louis Browns, 1888

World Series program cover, 1931

"The Gas House Gang," St. Louis Cardinals, 1934

Tim McCarver, Ken Boyer, and Bob Gibson celebrate after Game Seven victory, 1964 World Series

Whitey Kurowski, Enos Slaughter, and Johnny Beazley, 1942 World Champions

Cardinals celebrate after Game Seven victory, 1982 World Series

Cardinals celebrate championship, 2006 World Series

The 1940s set forth a strange rhythm of prosperity and a lack thereof for the Cardinals. In the wake of the bountiful war years, the team went throughout the 1950s without a pennant. Following the 1946 championship, the Cardinals did not claim another National League flag or World Series win until 1964. Schoendienst took over as manager after the 1964 championship, and a roster featuring Bob Gibson, Steve Carlton, Lou Brock, Orlando Cepeda, Roger Maris, Curt Flood, and Tim McCarver won pennants in 1967 and 1968.

The dynasty of the 1960s gave way to another long dry spell. Although Schoendienst's teams finished strong in several seasons during the 1970s, it was not until Whitey Herzog arrived as manager in 1980 that St. Louis began its rise back to the top, with teams built on speed and defense. Capturing pennants in 1982, 1985, and 1987, the Cardinals were the only major league team to play in three World Series during the decade, though they came out victorious in only 1982.

It's easy to assume that since Joe Torre followed Herzog in launching the 1990s for the Cards, the organization's success did not miss a beat. This was not the case, however, as the Redbirds went a full decade without a pennant. Tony La Russa took over the reins in 1996 and gradually built a winner. A veteran of postseason leadership with the Chicago White Sox and the Oakland A's, La Russa led St. Louis to seven postseason appearances in his first 11 seasons on the job, culminating in a long-awaited world championship in 2006. The 2004 team won 105 games—second most in club history, behind the 1942 squad—but lost to the Boston Red Sox in the World Series.

The World Series

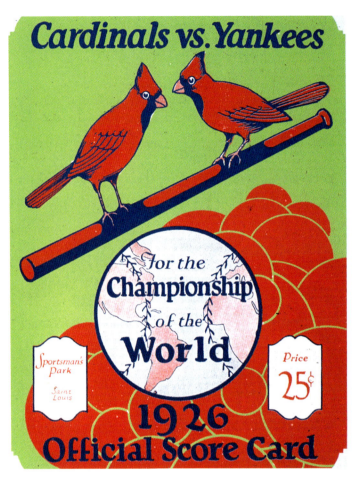
1926 World Series program

Babe Ruth and Rogers Hornsby shake hands before the 1926 World Series

The rich history of the Cardinals has often been displayed on the bright lights of the October stage. Although the modern World Series did not come into existence until 1903, the American Association's pennant-winning Browns teams of the 1880s took on the National League champs in postseason exhibitions. In 1885, Charles Comiskey's Browns split a seven-game series with Cap Anson's White Stockings. The opening game of that contest ended in a tie due to darkness, and in Game Two, the Browns players walked off the field in protest of an umpire's call, and Chicago was granted the win by forfeit. Although the series ended with three wins for each side, many Browns supporters insisted that they were the rightful winners because the forfeited second game should not have counted. The same two teams met again in the 1886 postseason exhibition, and this time St. Louis secured a non-controversial victory, winning four games to two.

The 1887 series was a marathon 15-game series that was played in nine different cities in an effort to spread the sport's appeal. The Detroit Wolverines defeated St. Louis 10 games to 5 in what was the first of four different decades in which the cities of Detroit and St. Louis would face off in a baseball championship. The 1888 postseason saw the Browns fall to the New York Giants in a best-of-10 series.

Following the 1888 pennant, St. Louis experienced a long, 37-year championship drought. The first pennant in the modern era of postseason play came in 1926, making the Cardinals the last of the eight National League franchises to play in a World Series. When they did finally get there, they faced a mighty New York Yankees team led by Babe Ruth and Lou Gehrig. Ruth hit three home runs in the fourth game of the series, in St. Louis, including one that cleared the Sportsman's Park bleachers and smashed the window of a car dealership across Grand Boulevard. That wasn't enough for the Bronx Bombers, though, and the Cardinals won

the seven-game series. The Yanks got their revenge two years later, sweeping the Cards in four straight games and outscoring them 27–10 in the 1928 Fall Classic.

A pennant in 1930 earned the Cardinals an October matchup with another dominating dynasty from the American League, Connie Mack's Philadelphia Athletics. Despite holding Philadelphia's powerful lineup to a .197 batting average in the series, St. Louis lost in six games. A year later, the two teams reunited in October, and this time outfielder Pepper Martin ran roughshod over the A's to give the Cards their second World Series title in franchise history. Martin stole five bases against Philadelphia's Hall of Fame catcher, Mickey Cochrane, while batting .500 in the seven-game series.

In 1934 against the Detroit Tigers, Martin again stepped up in October, scoring eight runs and posting a .355 average. The stars for St. Louis were brothers Dizzy and Paul Dean, who locked up the series with four complete-game victories between them. Dizzy, the elder Dean, won the opener and the deciding seventh game, while Paul, also known as "Daffy," allowed just two earned runs in 18 innings in Games Three and Six.

The Gas House Gang, 1934

Top: *Pepper Martin scores against Mickey Cochrane, Game Three, 1931 World Series*

Johnny Beazley being congratulated by Cardinals teammates after his Game Five win, 1942 World Series

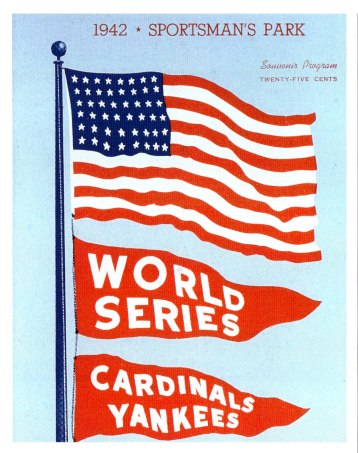

1942 World Series program

As the nation became embroiled in World War II, the Cardinals re-emerged as regular October participants on the baseball diamond. They encountered the star-filled Yankees of Joe DiMaggio, Bill Dickey, and Phil Rizzuto in the 1942 and 1943 World Series. St. Louis lost the opening game in 1942 and then won the next four. Rookie Johnny Beazley earned two complete-game victories in a span of four days, including the clinching fifth game, and fellow first-year player Whitey Kurowski delivered a two-run homer against Red Ruffing in the ninth inning of Game Five to help the Redbirds claim the championship three outs later. The Cardinals couldn't make it two titles in a row, however, and lost to New York in five games in 1943.

The 1944 Fall Classic pitted the Cardinals against the St. Louis Browns of the American League. The Browns, who like the Cardinals called Sportsman's Park home, were making their first World Series appearance in franchise history. The American League juniors were given a rude welcoming by the National Leaguers, who won in six games.

After Stan Musial and several other star Cardinals returned from military service, the team returned to the World Series for the fourth time in five years. They faced Ted Williams and the Boston Red Sox in 1946, and employed

Cardinals defense employing the "Williams Shift" against Ted Williams in Game One, 1946 World Series

an innovative defensive shift in an attempt to stymie the pull-hitting Williams. The Splendid Splinter was held to a .200 average in the series, and although Musial also hit well below his standards, Harry "The Hat" Walker picked up the slack and hit .412 while driving in six runs. Lefty Harry "The Cat" Brecheen won three games from the mound and allowed only one run in 20 innings. The pivotal moment of the series occurred in the eighth inning of Game Seven, when Enos Slaughter dashed all the way around from first base on a single by Walker to score the go-ahead run, as a startled Boston shortstop Johnny Pesky was unable to get a clean grip on the ball for his relay throw home.

Enos Slaughter scores on his "mad dash" in Game Seven, 1946 World Series

Another 18 seasons went by before the Cardinals returned to the Fall Classic. After a dramatic and nail-biting pennant race in 1964, the Cardinals encountered a new incarnation of the Yankees dynasty, featuring Mickey Mantle and Roger Maris. But the M&M Boys were little match for Bob Gibson, who tallied 33 strikeouts in 27 innings against New York's powerful lineup. After losing the opener, Gibson pitched a complete-game win in Game Five and did it again, on just two-days' rest, in Game Seven. A grand slam home run by Ken Boyer secured the victory in Game Four.

Gibson took it up another notch in 1967 against the Boston Red Sox, posting complete-game wins in Games One, Four, and Seven, and capping it off with a home run in the finale. The speedy Lou Brock collected 12 hits in the series and stole seven bases. Roger Maris, now in a Cardinals uniform, chipped in seven RBI.

St. Louis won a second straight pennant in 1968. Gibson again pitched every inning of all three games he started, and he set a World Series record with 17 strikeouts in Game One and 35 in the series. This time, though, the Redbirds and their ace pitcher failed to win the deciding seventh game against Detroit.

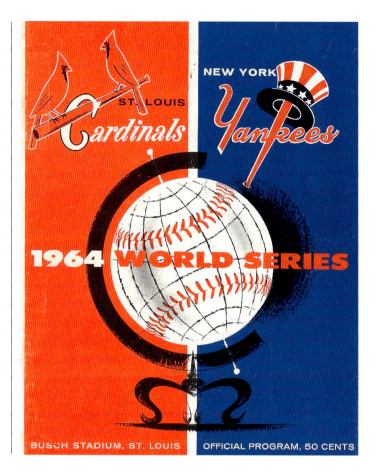

Ken Boyer scores after his grand slam in Game Four, 1964 World Series

When the Cardinals next appeared on the October stage, in 1982, the Whitey Herzog–led club built on speed and defense defeated the power-hitting Milwaukee Brewers in seven games. Rookie Willie McGee, who hit only four home runs all season, knocked two long balls in the third game of the series. In 1985, St. Louis lost a bitter battle against the cross-state rival Kansas City Royals. After a controversial, momentum-changing call by first base umpire Don Denkinger in Game Six (see the "Gaffes and Controversies" chapter), the Cardinals completely unraveled in Game Seven. In the 1987 World Series, the home team won each game, and the third Fall Classic appearance of the decade for the Cardinals—all against fellow Midwestern teams—ended with the Minnesota Twins claiming the title and another dose of disappointment for the Cardinals and their fans. It was the tenth time in 15 World Series trips that St. Louis needed all seven games to decide the outcome.

Right: *Bob Gibson, Game Seven, 1967 World Series*

Willie McGee at bat, 1982 World Series

The 2004 season, during which St. Louis won 105 games, also ended in disappointment with a four-game sweep at the hands of the Boston Red Sox. The 11–9 opener was the highest scoring Game One in World Series history, but the Cards managed a total of only three runs in the final three games. Although St. Louis' 83–78 record in 2006 marked the team's worst season in the new millennium, it ended well. Tony La Russa's crew outscored Detroit 22–11 in the five-game World Series to secure the franchise's tenth series title. Little David Eckstein brought home the series MVP Award for his clutch hitting and flawless fielding. He collected eight hits and four RBI in his final 11 at bats of the series.

David Eckstein, 2006 World Series

The 2006 world champion St. Louis Cardinals

Detroit fans pelt the field with debris, Game Seven, 1934 World Series

GAFFES AND CONTROVERSIES

Some of the strangest moments in Cardinals' history have surfaced in the postseason and particularly on baseball's biggest stage, the World Series.

Incensed at their team's inept play in Game Seven of the 1934 Fall Classic, the hometown Detroit Tigers' fans began to boil over with anger as the Cards led 9–0 in the sixth inning. At that point Joe Medwick, one of the St. Louis stars in the series, lashed a triple and slid hard into Tigers' third baseman Marv Owen. The two men tangled—perhaps inadvertently—as Medwick tried to get up, and then they faced off for a moment as the crowd hollered vociferously. When the Cards took their place in the field in the bottom half of the inning, order appeared to have been restored; but when Medwick jogged out to his position in left field, he was greeted with a shower of bottles, fruit, and other debris from the enraged Detroit onlookers in the bleachers.

"I watched the crowd and Medwick and the pelting missiles through my field glasses," reported writer Paul Gallico on the scene. "Every face in the crowd, women and men, was distorted with rage. Mouths were torn wide open, eyes glistened in the sun. All fists were clenched."

After nearly all of the left field area had been covered in garbage, Medwick and player-manager Frankie Frisch were summoned by Commissioner Kennesaw "Mountain" Landis, who was seated near the dugout. Landis ordered Medwick to leave the game for his own safety; many players and observers wondered what Landis would have done if the score had been closer. The Cardinals went on to win the game 11–0 and claimed the title in the process, with pitcher Dizzy Dean, much at Frisch's distress, using the closing moments to experiment with some new pitches.

Lou Brock attempting to score against Detroit catcher Bill Freehan, 1968 World Series

The Cardinals of the 1960s lived on speed and pitching. The running fueled their offense and fortified their defense, as star pitchers Bob Gibson, Steve Carlton, and others often relied on the team's fleet outfielders to chase down balls in the cavernous gaps of the new Busch Stadium, which opened for business in May 1966. Two of those outfielders in particular, Curt Flood and Lou Brock, seemed especially able to chase down any fly ball or outrun any tag on the bases with ease. At critical junctures, however, their skills momentarily failed each of them.

In Game Five of the 1968 World Series, in a rematch with the Tigers in Detroit, Brock steamed from second base, around third, and headed toward home plate, looking to score a run and add to the Cardinals' 3–2 lead. Surprised when Tigers catcher Bill Freehan suddenly appeared with the ball, Brock failed to slide around him, choosing instead to cross the plate standing up. Freehan tagged him out, and the Tigers went on to win the contest, 5–3. Three days later, in the seventh inning of Game Seven in St. Louis, Detroit's Jim Northrup batted a long fly ball toward Flood in center field. As sure at tracking flies as anyone in the game, Flood broke in on the ball, sensing that it was not hit very hard. He quickly realized that he had erred in judgment, stopped in his tracks, and tried to reverse himself to pursue the ball as it sailed over his head. He slipped and was unable to immediately regain his footing. Northrup zoomed into third base with a triple, and the Tigers tallied the first runs of the day. Detroit went on to win the game 4–1 and take the series in a four-games-to-three victory.

A date that lives in infamy with the Cardinals and their fans is October 26, 1985. The team appeared to be on its way to wrapping up a World Series victory against the Kansas City Royals. With the Cards holding a 1–0 lead in the bottom of the ninth inning, pitcher Danny Cox dashed over to cover the bag on a groundball to first baseman Jack Clark. Cox appeared to—and TV replays confirmed that he did—catch the ball from Clark and touch the first base bag with his foot in time to nab Royals batter Jorge Orta. However, American League umpire Don Denkinger called Orta safe, and the Royals took advantage of the extra out, rallying to win the game 2–1. The deflated Cardinals endured an 11–0 Game Seven drubbing the following night, and the Royals were crowned 1985 world champions. Pitcher Joaquin Andujar and manager Whitey Herzog were both ejected for arguing with the umpires during the finale.

Curt Flood making a great catch, 1964 World Series

Joaquin Andujar arguing with the umpire, Game Seven, 1985 World Series

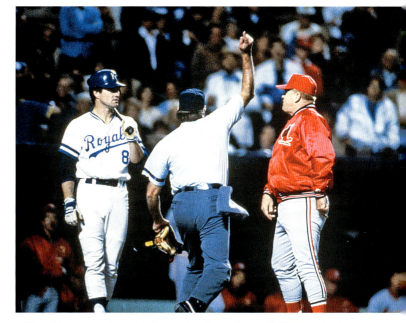
Whitey Herzog arguing with the umpire, Game Seven, 1985 World Series

The Rivalries

As the most successful franchise in National League history, the Cardinals have naturally developed several rivalries over the decades, by virtue of both geographical proximity and proximity in the league standings.

St. Louis was the first "small-market" city to have two major league teams within its boundaries—joining major metropolises New York, Boston, and Philadelphia—with the establishment of the American League Browns in St. Louis in 1902. (The Browns originated as the Milwaukee Brewers in 1901 but were relocated to St. Louis after one season.) Although the Browns would leave town in 1954 to become the Baltimore Orioles, for decades the taverns, bus stops, and streetcars of the Gateway City were alive with banter between followers of the Redbirds and backers of the lovable-loser Browns. Even with the disproportionate success that the Cardinals enjoyed on the field, the Brownies could always hold at least one thing over the Cards' heads: The deed to Sportsman's Park, where both teams played, was held in the name of the Browns organization, and the Redbirds were obligated to pay them rent. Because the teams shared an intra-city rivalry in the days before the introduction of interleague play to Major League Baseball, the only hope for the two squads to meet on the diamond, other than the occasional exhibition contest, was if they won the pennants of the respective leagues in the same season. Such an outcome seemed to be a highly unlikely prospect, considering that the Browns managed to finish higher than third place in the standings only twice in the first 43 seasons of the franchise's existence. The improbable became reality in 1944, when, with most major league rosters depleted by the demands of the military during World War II, the Browns seized the opportunity and finished at the top the American League at season's end. The Cardinals, meanwhile, secured a third consecutive pennant in the Senior Circuit, setting up a best-of-seven World Series to be played entirely within Sportsman's Park. In front of capacity crowds,

Missouri native Harry S. Truman with Browns manager Luke Sewell and Cardinals manager Billy Southworth, 1944 World Series

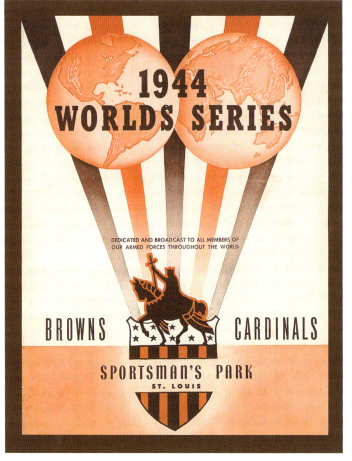

World Series program cover, 1944

the Browns jumped out to an early lead by winning the opener 2–1 and then capturing Game Three by the more convincing score of 6–2. But the veteran, postseason-tested Cardinals quickly regained control and outscored the Browns 10–2 over the next three contests to win the series in six games. It was the one and only appearance in the Fall Classic for the Browns.

The next time the Cardinals played in October against teams with a geographical connection was during the 1980s, when they faced off against three different Midwestern clubs in the World Series: Milwaukee, Kansas City, and Minnesota. The 1985 contest, dubbed the "I-70 Series" or "Show-Me Series," pitted the Cards against their cross-state mates from Kansas City. The Royals won the controversy-filled series in seven games.

First inning of Game One, 1944 World Series

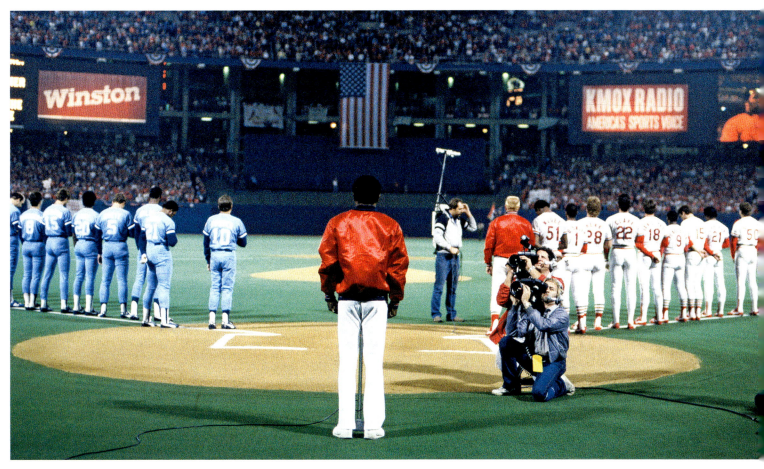

St. Louis Cardinals and Kansas City Royals lining up before Game Three of the 1985 World Series

Cardinals and Dodgers brawling at Sportsman's Park, August 1943

While the Cardinals have had occasional local rivals to battle in October, it may be argued that the franchise's most intense rivalries were with clubs based nearly a thousand miles away: the New York Giants and the Brooklyn Dodgers. The battles with the Giants were particularly fierce in the mid-1930s, when both teams were vying for pennants. In 1934, the Cards dethroned the defending world champion Giants, and Dizzy Dean and New York's player-manager Bill Terry regularly agitated each other throughout the season. The following spring, Diz hit four Giants batters in a row to start an exhibition game, before Terry insisted to the umpires that he be removed. By the end of the decade, each team could claim three National League pennants during the 1930s.

Prior to the 1940s, the Cards and Dodgers rarely had reason to be at odds, since the two teams were almost never in the pennant hunt at the same time. When former Gas House Gang shortstop Leo Durocher became the Dodgers' player-manager in late 1939, however, a new intensity was injected into the match-ups. Durocher brought winning ways back to Brooklyn, and in 1941 his "Bums"

Dodgers players congratulating the Cardinals following the 2004 National League Division Series

Cardinals Hall of Famer Frankie Frisch and Cubs Hall of Famer Gabby Hartnett, circa 1938

Albert Pujols and Chicago's Derrek Lee, 2005

Sammy Sosa and Mark McGwire, 1999

edged out Billy Southworth's Cards by three games, 100 wins to 97. The Cardinals turned the tables in 1942, winning the pennant by two games. The 1946 season ended with the two teams posting identical 96–58 records, requiring a best-of-three playoff to decide the league crown. The Cards won the first game at home and then defeated the Dodgers at Ebbets Field, and Brooklyn would have to wait until next year for another taste of the pennant. Although the relocation of the Dodgers to Los Angeles and the later realignment of the National League into two divisions put additional distance between the teams, they did have occasional opportunities to revive the old rivalry in the postseason. When the Cardinals captured the East Division title and the Dodgers won the West in 1985, St. Louis pulled out a dramatic victory in the League Championship Series, sparked by an unlikely home run by Ozzie Smith in Game Five.

Despite the long history with the Giants and Dodgers, no Cardinal rival has been more prominent, geographically and competitively, than the Chicago Cubs. Labeled "The I-55 Series" by authors Jim Rygelski and George Castle, the Cards-Cubs epic has had more than its share of classic moments. For Chicagoans, perhaps nothing was sweeter than the 1935 pennant chase, when the Cubs won an amazing 21 games in a row in September to take the pennant, a streak that culminated in wins over Dizzy and Paul Dean in St. Louis during the season-ending series between the teams. A modern, individualistic form of the rivalry took flight in 1998, when Mark McGwire of the Cardinals and Sammy Sosa of the Cubs thrilled audiences with their historic home-run chase.

With the fan loyalty base changing gradually as one traverses the state of Illinois north to south and south to north, the followers of both teams regularly fill the enemy's ballpark with the visitors' colors. And while the Cardinals hold an obvious advantage in pennants and World Series claimed, the Cubs hold the all-time lead in the head-to-head series: 1,146 wins to 1,078 for the Cards through 2008.

The Owners

It may surprise some to learn that August "Gussie" Busch Jr. was not the first St. Louis man associated with beer to own the Cardinals. The team's founder, Chris Von der Ahe, was the proprietor of a saloon in town and purchased the struggling baseball franchise in 1882. He entered it into the professional league known as the American Association. Knowing little about baseball, Von der Ahe merely saw ownership of the team as a way to expand his beverage business. After a fire at the home ballpark, a divorce from his wife, and other financial problems, Von der Ahe sold the team in 1898. The name was soon changed from the Browns to the Perfectos, and then the Cardinals in 1900 as the team entered the National League.

Chris Von der Ahe, Old Judge cigarettes baseball card, circa 1887

Von der Ahe was succeeded by Stanley Robison, and thereafter Robison's niece Schuyler Britton and a vacillation of other owners until 1920, when Sam Breadon finally offered a stable measure of controlling stock in the club. Breadon, coupled with his equally shrewd general manger Wesley "Branch" Rickey, knew that times were tough during the Great Depression, and he was not afraid to make his players share in the misery. As an example, he asked shortstop Leo Durocher to accept a $5,000 salary for 1934—nearly 40 percent less than he had made the previous year. Breadon's long tenure as club owner was followed in 1947 by the short stint of Robert Hannegan and Fred Saigh, who would have the team for six years, with Hannegan ultimately relinquishing all of his shares to Saigh.

Somewhat contrasting the penny-pinching style of Breadon was the oft-forgotten generous approach of Busch, who purchased the team in 1953 for $3.75 million (including $1.25 million of the club's debt). Busch also acquired the property title to Sportsman's Park from the Browns, as the other St. Louis club was leaving town to become the Baltimore Orioles. Busch was such a reversal from previous Cardinals owners in his willingness to spend money that he became incensed after realizing that he could not simply buy away other teams' stars. This is demonstrated by his disbelief with the Cubs owner at the time, Phillip K. Wrigley, who in the late 1950s refused Busch's offer to purchase Chicago shortstop Ernie Banks for $500,000. Why, Busch wanted to know, did the deal not go through? "Uh, Mr. Busch," one of his advisers reminded him, "Mr. Wrigley needs half a million dollars about as much as you do."

Schuyler Britton and her husband, 1913

Stanley Robison, 1909

Sam Breadon (center) with manager Gabby Street (left) and captain Frankie Frisch, 1931

August A. Busch Jr. (right) with Fred Saigh announcing the sale of the Cardinals to Anheuser-Busch, February 1953

August Busch Jr. (center) with manager Eddie Stanky, Enos Slaughter, Red Schoendienst, and Stan Musial at spring training, March 1953

Curt Flood at the Federal Court building in New York, June 1970

Gussie Busch followed his beloved Cardinals very closely, often going on long train rides to trail the team from city to city. The slow trips offered the opportunity for a series of rousing, lengthy card games with his friends—who were admonished by Busch when they asked train porters for a beer and not a Budweiser specifically.

Busch continued to be kind with his own players, paying them handily. The 1968 Cards became famous with their depiction on the cover of *Sports Illustrated* in October that year as the "Million-Dollar Club." It was the founding of the Major League Baseball Players Association earlier in the decade, however, that helped to foster a newfound boldness among players in regard to money and contracts, with St. Louis' Curt Flood leading the charge by refusing to report to training camp in 1969. This enraged Busch, and he stormed into the team's clubhouse in spring training that year and berated the general greediness of the modern ballplayer. Busch felt that he had been most supportive of Flood, his family, and the other players over the years, and he was hurt that the outfielder would hold out for what he considered to

August Busch Jr. throwing out the ceremonial first pitch, 1982 World Series

be an exorbitant sum. Flood was quickly packaged in a trade to Philadelphia, but he refused to report to the Phillies. Flood contended that Major League Baseball's reserve clause, which perpetually bound a player to one team without competitive negotiation from other teams, was illegal, but his challenge was rejected by the U.S. Supreme Court in 1970. Several years later, though, an arbitrator ruled that the reserve clause offered clubs only a single year of additional service, and thus the groundwork for modern-day free agency was formed.

Busch passed away in 1989, and in late 1995 Anheuser-Busch illustrated its desire to focus on its core business by selling several assets. The Cardinals were sold to a consortium of businesspeople, including current chairman and principal owner Bill DeWitt Jr., for approximately $150 million. Under DeWitt's leadership, the team reasserted its place among the National League elite.

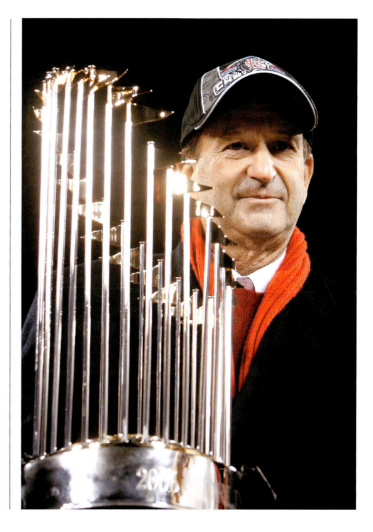

William Dewitt Jr. with World Series trophy, October 2006

The General Managers

"Never try to jilt the other guy in a trade," Branch Rickey always advised, "because someday, you might want to go back and deal with that guy again." Rickey would occasionally raise the ire of Cardinals fans by trading players in the prime of their careers—which is exactly what he intended to do. "Never trade a guy on the downside of his career," he added to his long list of maxims, "and always acquire a guy on his upside." By the time he was serving Sam Breadon as essentially the first general manager in baseball history in the 1930s, Rickey was well on his way to procuring talent for his team in a manner that none had ever witnessed before. Knowing that the cash-strapped Cardinals could not compete with the wealthier clubs of the East Coast, Rickey applied the wartime domestic strategy of food rationing to the world of baseball: He decided to "grow" his own in a revolutionary farm system. With numerous understudies of players on teams throughout the country, the Cardinals could cultivate their own players, to be brought to the parent club as they were ready for "the Show."

Vaughan "Bing" Devine loved the Cardinals ever since his days growing up on the streets of St. Louis and through his days at University City High School and Washington University, both in St. Louis. He rose to become the team's general manger in 1957, but his moves were not always viewed as favorable by the players, at least at the outset. One such incident occurred on June 15, 1964, when the Cardinals acquired the erratic but talented outfield prospect Lou Brock from the Chicago Cubs in exchange for pitcher Ernie Broglio. Heading into the 1964 season, Broglio had won 60 games for St. Louis over the previous four years, and fellow hurler Bob Gibson was initially dismayed that Devine would part with an established starting pitcher for an untested position player. With the Cards mired in the second division with a 28–31 record on the date of the trade, Devine was convinced that such a jumpstart was necessary. His belief held true, as Brock batted .348 the rest of the way for the Cardinals (after hitting .251 until June 15 with the Cubs). He also added a new measure of speed to the team, nabbing 33 stolen bases in those 103 final games of 1964. Brock was integral to bringing the Cards their first league pennant and World Series win in nearly two decades—and so originated a long career in a Redbirds uniform for the swift Louisiana native. Broglio, meanwhile, struggled to a 4–7 record with the Cubs for the remainder of 1964 and was out of baseball in two years.

Devine held the post of general manager until the end of that season, when he was fired by Gussie Busch for allegedly

Branch Rickey, circa 1922

Branch Rickey watching Joe Medwick sign a new contract, 1939

Bing Devine with Lou Brock after re-signing the player, 1968

conspiring behind the owner's back with field manager Johnny Keane about club transactions. Busch intended to fire Keane as well, and replace him with Leo Durocher; however, after Keane led the Cardinals to the 1964 championship, Busch changed his mind and offered Keane a new contract. Busch, however, had the tables turned on him for one of the few times in his professional life, when the manager announced suddenly in a post-series press conference that he was leaving town to manage the Yankees. After short stints by Bob Howsam, Stan Musial, and even Rickey once again, Devine returned to the Cardinals for a second turn at the general manager's helm, a post he held until 1978 when he was replaced by John Claiborne.

Bing Devine, circa 1963

Whitey Herzog in his office, 1981

Walt Jocketty (left) with manager Tony La Russa, 2002

In 1980, Whitey Herzog was brought aboard as both general manager and field manager. That season, Herzog temporarily turned over the controls in the dugout to Red Schoendienst so he could devote his time to procuring the precise talent he sought for the club. Immediately, his eyes fell upon a young infielder in San Diego named Ozzie Smith.

By the end of the 1981 season, there was no question that switch-hitting shortstop Garry Templeton was establishing himself as a bona fide offensive threat. In 1979, he had become the first player in major league history to get 100 hits from each side of the plate in one season. However, his inconsistent glove work at this critical defensive position—Templeton committed an average of 32 errors per season in his first five years with the team—caused much angst for Cardinals officials and fans. On December 10, 1981, Templeton was sent to the San Diego Padres along with outfielder Sixto Lezcano for Smith and pitcher Steve Mura. While Smith's batting numbers paled in comparison to Templeton's, the Cardinals felt that they were acquiring a player who was emerging as one of the best defensive shortstops the game had seen in some time. Herzog soon made other deft moves in building the team he desired, such as acquiring promising outfielder Willie McGee from the New York Yankees in a 1981 trade for the nominal price of pitcher Bob Sykes.

Having established himself as a reliable and intelligent player in the 1960s, Dal Maxvill returned to the Cardinals to serve

John Mozeliak (left) at the first-year player draft in Florida, 2007

as the club's general manager from 1985 to 1994, relieving Joe McDonald and helping in Herzog's continued ascension to two more National League pennants after a world championship in 1982. Like Devine, Maxvill was a graduate of local Washington University and was widely respected for his intellectual approach to player-personnel decisions.

Just before Busch's sale of the club and Tony La Russa's arrival as manager in St. Louis was the hiring of Walt Jocketty, who took Maxvill's place as general manager in October 1994. Jocketty had earned his stripes toiling for 14 years in the Oakland A's organization, working the minor league system and in the scouting department. He wished to bring La Russa to St. Louis along with him and attempt to mirror the success that the A's had enjoyed in the late 1980s. While in St. Louis, Jocketty orchestrated a number of moves that helped produce seven playoff appearances for the Cardinals during his term. When grand slugger Mark McGwire went down with an injury in 2000, Jocketty picked up longtime all-star Will Clark to fill the void. After getting a hit in his first St. Louis at-bat on August 1, Clark went on to homer in his next four games. He batted .345 in 51 games for the Cardinals in the final two months of that season, Clark's final contests in a major league uniform.

After moving on to assist the Cincinnati Reds in an advisory capacity in January 2008 (much as Rickey had done when he returned to the Cardinals for the last time in the 1960s), Jocketty was elevated to the position of the Reds' general manager within a matter of months. He was replaced in St. Louis by John Mozeliak, who had served as Jocketty's assistant general manager for five years.

George Crowe (right) and Stan Musial at spring training, 1960

Breaking the Race Barrier

In January 1954, the Cardinals acquired Tom Alston from the San Diego Padres of the Pacific Coast League, and three months later, on April 13, he made his major league debut. Although his big-league career lasted only 91 games over four seasons, Alston was etched into the annals of Cardinals history by becoming the first African American to play for the franchise. Thirty-six-year-old George Crowe joined the team in 1959 and played limited duty as a first baseman and pinch hitter for two seasons while establishing a model of leadership for African-American players.

A decade after Alston's debut, a diverse cast in St. Louis defeated the New York Yankees in the 1964 World Series. The Cardinals were among the first major league teams to fully integrate their roster with players from various races. By 1964, Bob Gibson, Curt Flood, and Bill White were the unquestioned

Mike Gonzalez, circa 1934

leaders on the team; Lou Brock joined the club in midseason 1964 following a trade with the Chicago Cubs.

The core of Gibson, Flood, White, and Brock jelled almost seemlessly with established white stars such as Ken Boyer, Dick Groat, Mike Shannon, and Tim McCarver. Dominican-born second baseman Julian Javier joined St. Louis as a 23-year-old rookie in 1960, and in October 1963 he took part in the only Hispanic Major League All-Star Game ever played, held in the Polo Grounds in New York. While not quite achieving the fame of Jimmy Durante singing "Cha-Cha-Cha," the "El Birdos" ditty became a popular theme song for the Cardinals during the magical summers of 1967 and 1968 due to the Hispanic influence of Javier and Puerto Rican–born Orlando Cepeda.

The Cardinals' history of diversity, however, stretches long before the 1960s. Mike Gonzalez, a native of Havana, Cuba, played catcher and first base for St. Louis from 1915 to 1918 and later served as an assistant coach under manager Frankie Frisch in the 1930s. Gonzalez filled in as interim skipper for 16 games at the end of the 1938 season, making him the first foreign-born player to manage in the major leagues. The Cardinals organization is also credited with having the first Australian-born player in the majors: Joe Quinn, who was on the roster at various times in the 1890s.

About a century later, pitcher Rene Arocha followed Gonzalez's lead by helping to launch a new wave of talent coming to the United States from Cuba. Colombia native Edgar Renteria solidified the

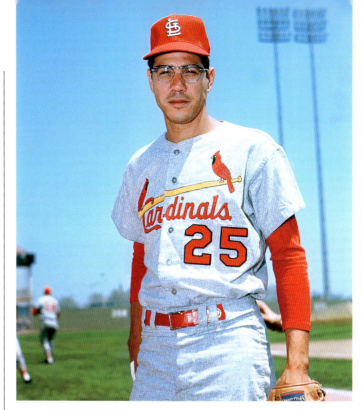

Julian Javier, circa 1964

Cards' shortstop position from 1999 to 2004—only the third major leaguer in that country's history. In 2002, outfielder So Taguchi brought to St. Louis skills that were nurtured in his home country of Japan. The 2006 World Series champions featured Puerto Rican native Yadier Molina behind the plate, Dominicans Albert Pujols at first and Juan Encarnacion in right, and Taguchi in left.

So Taguchi (right) and Juan Encarnacion, 2007

Miller Huggins (left) with New York Giants manager John McGraw and umpire Bill Brennan, 1913

The Managers

Charles Comiskey, Allen & Ginter cigarettes baseball card, 1887

Those who study early Cardinals history may be surprised to learn that some of baseball's more famous front-office men got their start on the playing field. As the star first baseman of the St. Louis Browns of the American Association in the 1880s, Charles Comiskey took over the managerial role late in his second year with the club, in 1883, at the age of 23. Comiskey led the team to four straight AA titles starting in 1885, including an 1886 world championship series win over the Chicago White Stockings. (In later years, Comiskey became the famously gruff and tightfisted owner of the American League's Chicago White Sox and endured Chicago's scandalous 1919 season, when the Sox were accused of throwing the World Series.)

That same year, a 37-year-old former catcher named Branch Rickey took over as manager of the Cardinals. Although he posted a .239 career batting average in four nondescript seasons as a big league player, Rickey earned his first managerial job at the age of 31 with the St. Louis Browns of the American League in 1913. He held the manager's job with the Cards from 1919 until 1925, when he handed the reins to star second

Bill McKechnie, 1928

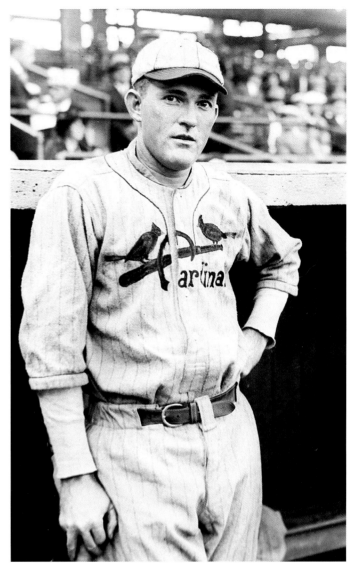

Rogers Hornsby, 1926

baseman Rogers Hornsby so that Rickey could focus his efforts in the team's front office.

Prior to Rickey, another second baseman ran the show in the Cardinals dugout: Miller Huggins. A decent player—he led the league with a .432 on-base percentage in 1913—Huggins would earn his Hall of Fame credentials as manager of great New York Yankee teams in the 1920s. As skipper of the Cards from 1913 to 1917, Huggins experienced just two winning seasons.

As player-manager, Hornsby led the Cardinals to a World Series win in 1926, and after Hornsby was shipped off to the Giants in 1927, catcher Bob O'Farrell did double duty as manager for one season. Hall of Fame skipper Bill McKechnie took them to the World Series in 1928, and the team employed a trio of helmsmen in 1929—McKechnie, Billy Southworth, and Gabby Street—before Street got the full-time job in 1930.

Charles "Gabby" Street—like Rickey a former major league catcher—led the team to back-to-back pennants in his first two seasons as skipper and went on to defeat Connie Mack's Philadelphia A's in the 1931 World Series. Street's star second baseman was Frankie Frisch, who despite being a great player in his own right had the unfortunate task of replacing the legendary Rogers Hornsby at the position, and thus needed to work hard to endear himself to Cardinals fans. By mid-1933, Frisch had proven his worth sufficiently to owner Sam Breadon that he was named player-manager. Frisch went on to lead the Gas House Gang to the title in this capacity in 1934.

A slight lull hit the Cardinals in the National League standings in the late 1930s, but the trend was reversed in 1940 with the hiring of Billy Southworth as manager. Southworth

Gabby Street (left) with New York Giants manager John McGraw, 1931

Frankie Frisch, 1937

had served as a player-manager for the Cardinals for 90 games during the 1929 season, just before Street settled in to lead the club. In his five full seasons as manager (1941–1945), Southworth led St. Louis to 508 wins, three straight National League pennants, and World Series victories in 1942 and 1944. His .642 career winning percentage is the highest among all Cardinal skippers since Comiskey.

Eddie Dyer followed Southworth in 1946, and although he managed the Cards to another title that year, he would never again reach those heights in his next four seasons on the job. Dyer was succeeded by a string of ex-players that included Marty Marion, Eddie Stanky, and Harry Walker. Former infielder Solly Hemus led the team from the end of the 1950s into the 1960s, but he was out of the picture by the time the team had reasserted itself as a consistent contender.

During the 1960s, the Cardinals turned to men long loyal to the organization to lead the club on the field. First was Johnny Keane, who spent 24 years in the Cards' minor league system as a player and manager before getting a chance with the big league club. He was handed the reins midway through the 1961 season and went on to guide the Redbirds to 93-win seasons in 1963 and 1964. After leading the club to triumph in the 1964 World Series, Keane abruptly left town to manage the Yankees—the team he had just defeated in the seven-game series.

Billy Southworth (left) with rookie Stan Musial at spring training, 1942

Eddie Dyer (right) with pitcher Max Lanier, 1949

Right: *Johnny Keane arguing with an umpire, 1964 World Series*

Left: *Red Schoendienst with Curt Flood, 1968*

Below: *Whitey Herzog talking with an umpire, 1982 World Series*

Joe Torre, 1990

Tony La Russa arguing with the umpires, 2007

Following Keane's departure, coach Red Schoendienst shifted into the managerial role. A native of nearby Germantown, Illinois, and longtime Cardinal second baseman, Schoendienst immediately commanded the respect of his charges with his impeccable character and knowledge of the game. The team won more than 1,000 games during his 12-year tenure from 1965 to 1976 (he returned for brief stints as interim manager in 1980 and 1990), and in 1967, he became the seventh different Cardinals manager to take the franchise to the promised land of World Series victory. Schoendienst also oversaw the Cards' evolution from a slugging outfit to a dominant running team, and thus set the stage for the speedy and successful teams of the next decade.

With the exception of 89 games in 1980, Whitey Herzog managed the Cardinals in every game during the decade of the 1980s, plus 80 more games in 1990, leading the team to three pennants in the process. Herzog was followed by yet another household name in the managerial business, as well as in team history, Joe Torre. The former St. Louis catcher and infielder was making his third stint as a big league skipper, following terms with the New York Mets and Atlanta Braves, when he stepped into the Cardinals job on August 1, 1990. Torre's Redbirds posted three straight winning seasons before tumbling below the .500 mark in the strike-shortened 1994 campaign. After the team got off to a slow start in 1995, Torre was fired as manager.

Following the sale of the team by Anheuser-Busch at the end of 1995, the Cardinals turned to Tony La Russa to forge another run of postseason success. La Russa did not disappoint. He led the team to the top of the National League Central Division in his first season in St. Louis and followed that with five more division crowns, two pennants, and one World Series title through 2008. La Russa has won more games as Cardinals manager than anybody else in the history of the franchise.

CATCHERS

With a few exceptions, catchers for the Cardinals have produced only modest offensive numbers but have nonetheless played vital roles with their defense behind the plate and as leaders in the clubhouse.

Neither of the backstops on St. Louis' championship teams of the 1880s did much to distinguish themselves. Doc Bushong was a .214 lifetime hitter who posted a career-high .267 average in 1885 before dipping to .223 the following year. Jack Boyle came on the scene in 1887 and batted a meager .189, which he upped to .241 for the 1888 pennant season.

The Cardinals did have a Hall of Famer doing time at catcher from 1909 to 1912, but Roger Bresnahan's Cooperstown credentials were established primarily during his previous tenure with the New York Giants. Bresnahan also served as the team manager during his four seasons in St. Louis.

Early in the 1925 season, the Cardinals received catcher Bob O'Farrell in a trade with the Cubs, and O'Farrell went on to be named the National League Most Valuable Player in 1926. O'Farrell batted .293 that year, far from the highest mark on his own team, but his leadership behind the plate helped catapult the club to the pennant. He went on to catch every pitch for St. Louis in that year's World Series and threw out Babe Ruth trying to steal second base for the final out in the seven-game series.

The Cardinals' first longtime star at catcher was Jimmie Wilson, who arrived in St. Louis from the Philadelphia Phillies in May 1928. The next year Wilson batted .325 and posted career highs with 71 RBI, 59 runs, 128 hits, and a .464 slugging percentage. Following an all-star season in 1933, Wilson was sent back to the Phillies in exchange for fellow backstop Virgil "Spud" Davis—who had gone to Philadelphia from St. Louis in the trade for Wilson five years earlier. At 6-foot-1 and 200 pounds, Davis was a relatively large target, and Cardinals hurlers loved to throw to his big, soft hands. He batted over .300 in his first two seasons with St. Louis, providing a balanced force at the plate and in the field.

Behind the dish for the latter part of the 1930s was Mickey Owen, a native of southwest Missouri who brought more athleticism to the position than any who came before him in St. Louis. Owen was among the first catchers to throw to second base from a squatting position. As with Leo Durocher, Joe Medwick, and others, Mickey Owen was coveted by Branch Rickey, and after Rickey left the Cardinals for the Dodgers, the catcher became a key member of Durocher's Brooklyn club in 1941. After his baseball days were over, Owen returned to the area where he grew up, near Springfield, Missouri, to become the sheriff of Greene County. He also established the Mickey Owen Baseball School in 1959, which is still in operation as one of the country's best facilities for youth baseball instruction.

Doc Bushong, Gold Coin Chewing Tobacco baseball card, 1887

Roger Bresnahan, 1911

Jimmie Wilson blocking the plate against Al Simmons, 1931 World Series

Cardinals catchers Herman Franks, Mickey Owen, Don Padgett, and Sam Narron, 1939

Walker Cooper (left) with brother Mort Cooper, 1943 World Series

Though Walker Cooper's tenure in St. Louis was brief (1941–1944), he was there for one of the most successful runs in franchise history. Cooper was an all-star catcher for the Cardinals in all three pennant seasons during World War II, and he batted .305 over that span. He bounced around to several other teams before returning to St. Louis in 1956 and then retired the following season at the age of 42. Cooper's older brother Mort was the Cardinals' ace pitcher during their championship runs in the early 1940s.

Del Rice and his partner behind the plate, St. Louis native Joe Garagiola, worked the lean years of the late 1940s and early 1950s, and Hal Smith earned two all-star selections during his turn in the second half of the 1950s. But this trio, as well as a few other, lesser known catchers, were simply holding down the position until Tim McCarver came on the scene as a 17-year-old prospect out of Memphis, Tennessee. A star in football as well as baseball in high school, McCarver turned down football scholarship offers from Notre Dame and other schools and instead accepted a large signing bonus from the Cardinals in 1959. Four years later, he was the team's starting catcher at the age of 21. McCarver was consistent with the bat, hitting between .274 and .295 in every season from 1963 to 1967 and driving in an average of 58 runs. He also led the league in triples, a rare feat for a catcher, in 1966. McCarver batted .478 and drove in five runs during the 1964 World Series victory over the Yankees but lost out to his star pitcher, Bob Gibson, for series MVP honors. McCarver was also behind the plate for the 1967 and 1968 pennants. In 1967, he posted career highs with 14 homers, 69 RBI, .295 average, and .452 slugging percentage. Ending his career with the Phillies in 1980, McCarver played major league baseball in four different decades. (He appeared in eight games for the Cardinals in 1959 after signing his initial contract.)

While McCarver was still firmly entrenched as the Redbirds' catcher in 1968, and still just 26 years old, the club nonetheless knew that it needed to look toward the future. In doing so, they selected the switch-hitting Ted Simmons out of high school with their first pick in the 1967 amateur draft. In an era of great catchers, Simmons was unquestionably among the top of the list for batting production at the position in the 1970s. After assuming the full-time starter's job in 1971, he bested the .300 mark seven times in ten seasons and twice drove in more than 100 runs while with St. Louis. A six-time all-star in a Cardinals uniform, Simmons exhibited decent home run power and belted 20 or more dingers five times. His 1,439 games behind the plate for St. Louis are tops in franchise history.

Left: *Tim McCarver, 1967 World Series*

Below: *Ted Simmons tagging out New York Met John Stearns, circa 1979*

Less than a week before trading Simmons to Milwaukee in December 1980, the Cardinals signed free-agent catcher Darrell Porter. A former all-star with the Brewers and Royals, Porter spent five years with St. Louis, including the 1982 and 1985 pennant seasons. Following Porter's release after the 1985 season, the Redbirds turned away from offensive-minded catchers and opted for players with strong throwing arms and other defensive skills to contend with the onset of the intense running game in the National League in the 1980s (which to a large extent was propagated by the Cardinals).

Quality backstops such as Tom Nieto, Tony Pena, and Tom Pagnozzi took their turns behind the plate at Busch Stadium, looking to stem the onslaught of opponents in the stolen base–happy decade. A three-time Gold Glove Award winner with Pittsburgh, Pena batted a mere .214 for the pennant-winning Cardinals in 1987, but he threw out nearly one-third of all runners attempting to steal during his three seasons in St. Louis.

Darrell Porter, 1982 World Series

Tom Pagnozzi, 1992

Mike Matheny

Yadier Molina

Pagnozzi, who started as a backup in 1987, enjoyed the longest tenure during this period. Despite a modest .253 career batting average, Pagnozzi's skills as a catcher were good enough for a 12-year major league career, all with the Cardinals, and three Gold Glove Awards.

After a couple of seasons witnessing the versatile Eli Marrero behind the plate, Cardinals fans in the post-Pagnozzi era would have the pleasure of watching Mike Matheny ply his trade at the catcher's post from 2000 to 2004. As with Pagnozzi and other Redbirds at the position, Matheny's offensive production was limited, as he would never hit higher than .261 in his five seasons as a Cardinal. Even so, his defensive performance was unmatched among National League catchers of the time, and Matheny brought home three Gold Gloves while with St. Louis and added another with the San Francisco Giants in 2005.

Yadier Molina—one of three catching Molina brothers from Puerto Rico—took over for Matheny in 2005 and has steadily improved his game each season. His batting average jumped to .304 in 2008, and he struck out only 29 times in 444 at bats. Molina was also a key piece in the title run of 2006, driving in six runs in the NLCS and batting .412 in the World Series. The Cardinals will continue to look for Molina to capitalize on his enormous potential and mature into the type of leader that McCarver, Pagnozzi, and Matheny were before him.

First Basemen

As with many National League teams over the decades, Cardinals first basemen have often stood as the main power source on the team, adding a home run threat to an offense that was often fueled by stolen bases and hit-and-run execution.

In the early years of the franchise, however—an era when home runs were more often accomplished with balls hit inside the park rather than over the fences—first baseman Charles Comiskey had a penchant for speed on the base paths. Comiskey stole 419 bases in 13 major league seasons, nine of which were spent with the St. Louis Browns of the American Association (the Cardinals' forebear). While doing double-duty as manager for the league champs in 1887, Comiskey batted .335, knocked in 103 runs, scored 139 runs, and stole 117 bases.

"Big Ed" Konetchy (1907–1913) was also a threat to swipe a bag, stealing 148 of them during his years in a St. Louis uniform. He also finished among the top ten home run hitters in the league four times, but in those dead-ball days, his single-season peak for St. Louis was eight.

Charles Comiskey, Gold Coin Chewing Tobacco baseball card, 1887

Ed Konetchy, American Tobacco Company baseball card, 1911

Jim Bottomley, 1927

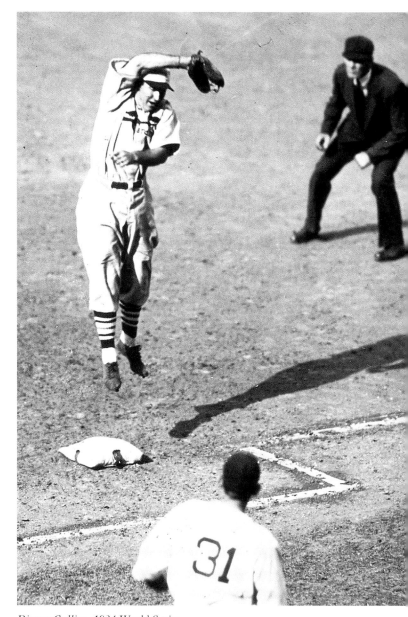

Ripper Collins, 1934 World Series

As the game evolved into its twentieth-century form during the 1920s, the Cardinals first sackers assumed the often-lone slugger's role in the lineup. Jack Fournier belted 16 homers while batting .343 in 1921, but it was his successor, Jim Bottomley, who truly embraced the role of extra-base threat at the position. A .325 hitter in his 11 seasons with the Cardinals (1922–1932), the future Hall of Famer posted most-impressive averages of .371 and .367 in 1923 and 1925, respectively, but lost out on the batting crown to teammate Rogers Hornsby both times. Bottomley peaked in 1928, when he captured the National League MVP Award with 42 doubles, 20 triples, 31 home runs, 123 runs, and 136 RBI.

Similarly gaudy numbers landed some MVP votes (and a sixth-place finish for the award) in 1934 for James "Ripper" Collins. With 35 homers, 128 RBI, and a .333 average, Collins stood as the main power source, along with Joe Medwick, for the world champion Gas House Gang. Although his stats were not as impressive, Collins earned all-star selections in each of the next two seasons before being traded to the Cubs in 1936.

Johnny Mize

The power surge at first base intensified with the emergence of Johnny Mize in 1936. At 6-foot-2 and 215 pounds, Mize was considered big for the 1930s and 1940s, but his "Big Cat" nickname was bestowed for his smooth, catlike play in the field and his beautiful swing at bat. While teammate Joe Medwick won the National League Triple Crown in 1937, Mize nearly pulled off the feat two years later, leading the circuit in batting average (.349) and home runs (28) but finishing third in RBI with 108. Although Mize's average dipped to its lowest point in his time with the Cardinals in 1940—to .314—his 43 homers and 137 RBI were tops in the National League, as he posted his second straight second-place finish in the MVP voting. Mize spent six seasons (1936–1941) in St. Louis before moving on to finish his Hall of Fame career in New York with the Giants and Yankees.

After Mize's departure, the Cardinals captured three straight pennants with Johnny Hopp and Ray Sanders at first base—fine ballplayers both of them, but not up to the standards of those who came before them, and certainly a far cry from "The Man" who would take the position next.

Stan Musial, warming up at first base, 1956

Bill White, 1960

Orlando Cepeda, 1968

Starting in 1946, the great Stan Musial was called upon to vacate his usual outfield position and take over first base responsibilities. He played there for most of 1946 and all of 1947 and then returned to the outfield for the better part of the next seven seasons. He was back on infield duty from 1955 through 1959 before again reassuming his preferred spot in the outer pastures for the final four years of his career. (Musial took his turns at first base begrudgingly, as he admitted to be much more comfortable farther away from the plate, in the outfield.)

During the later 1940s and early 1950s, the first base job was filled by the likes of Nippy Jones, Dick Sisler, and Steve Bilko, but when they acquired Giants castoff Bill White in 1959, stability at the position was restored. White was a five-time all-star and six-time Gold Glove Award winner at first base in St. Louis from 1960 to 1965. (He also earned an all-star invite while manning the outfield in 1959.) During those six Gold Glove seasons, White also contributed 20 or more homers five times and hit over .300 three times.

As with White, another trade with the San Francisco Giants brought a star first baseman to St. Louis. Orlando Cepeda arrived on the banks of the Mississippi River on May 8, 1966, as a member of the Cardinals' opponent that day, the Giants. After the game between the two teams that afternoon, however, Cepeda switched uniforms, locker rooms, and teammates, and he moved to the home side of the stadium in a trade that sent Redbirds pitcher Ray Sadecki to the Giants. Cepeda—known as "Cha-Cha"—quickly became a crowd favorite in St. Louis for his enthusiasm and his talent. Swinging one of the heaviest bats in the major leagues, Cepeda clubbed his way to the 1967 National League MVP Award, and he led the victory cheers in the locker room with shouts of *"Viva El Birdos!"* He played first base for the 1968 pennant winners as well before being traded to Atlanta for Joe Torre in the subsequent offseason.

Mark McGwire

Joe Torre filled Cepeda's position at first base for the 1969 season but spent the next three seasons as the team's third baseman, as well as some time at catcher. He returned to the left side of the infield in 1973 and 1974 and then was shipped to the New York Mets (in exchange for Ray Sadecki, no less) to make room for a young prospect named Keith Hernandez. A 42nd round draft choice by St. Louis in the 1971 amateur draft, Hernandez was considered too small (6 feet tall, 190 pounds) to hit for legitimate power in the major leagues. What he soon offered the team, however, was the slickest fielding first basemen since Mize and an ability to drive the ball into the alleys. At the age of 25 in 1979, Hernandez exploded with a National League–best .344 batting average (more than 50 points higher than any of his five previous major league seasons), 48 doubles, and 105 RBI, and like Cepeda before him, Hernandez brought home the MVP Award. He also won his

Keith Hernandez, 1979

Albert Pujols, 2008

second in what would be 11 consecutive Gold Glove Awards. He remained a fixture at first base until the middle of the 1983 season, when he was dealt to the New York Mets for pitchers Neil Allen and Rick Ownbey.

From 1985 to 1991, sluggers Jack Clark and Pedro Guerrero returned the first base position in St. Louis to one of home run power. Clark belted 35 homers in 1987 while leading the league in both on-base percentage and slugging percentage. The long-ball prowess of this pair, however, paled in comparison to the blasts emitted by the man who arrived in town on July 31, 1997, from the Oakland A's—Mark McGwire, or "Big Mac." McGwire had been an accomplished pitcher and hitter in his collegiate days at the University of Southern California, but his paycheck in the majors was derived from his ability to drive the ball over the fence.

McGwire Mania hit full throttle in St. Louis in midsummer 1998 when he was grappling with the Chicago Cubs' Sammy Sosa in pursuit of Roger Maris' single-season home run record—a record McGwire would own by season's end with 70. He knocked 65 more in 1999 and matched his RBI total of the previous season with 147. Eight years after his retirement in 2001, McGwire still held the career record for at bats per home run, slugging one every 10.6 official trips to the plate.

In McGwire's final season, a 21-year-old phenom from the Dominican Republic, Albert Pujols, joined the team and split his time between the outfield, third base, and first base. By 2004, he was the full-time first baseman, and he's been tearing up the league ever since. (His exploits are described in detail in the following section, "Hit Men.")

Hit Men

As the rookie pitcher winds up and hurls a fastball toward the middle of the plate, he is confident that he has gotten ahead of the hitter in the count. The umpire, however, remains motionless to indicate that the pitch was a ball. Disappointed, the rookie rears back once again and believes he has caught a portion of the plate. The umpire, again unimpressed, remains motionless to make the count 2–0.

Now disgusted, the brash rookie pitcher trudges halfway toward home plate, puts his hands on his hips, and glares at the arbiter, wanting to know why the calls did not go his way. The umpire takes a few steps toward him, calmly lifts his mask, and says quietly and politely, "Young man, *Mr. Hornsby* will let you know when you've thrown a strike."

This story—whether fact or legend—illustrates the reverence that Rogers Hornsby earned as one of baseball's great hitters. Often lauded as the greatest right-handed batter the game has ever seen, Hornsby batted over .400 three times between 1921 and 1925 (in addition to .397 and .384 marks in the other two seasons); led the league in batting average, slugging percentage, and on-base percentage in every season from 1920 to 1925; led the league in RBI four times in that same span; and collected more than 200 hits in a season five times. Hornsby won Triple Crowns in 1922 and 1925 by leading the league in average, RBI, and home runs, and he was named the National League Most Valuable Player in 1925— and surely would have won more had the award been in existence prior to 1924. A firestorm erupted in the press and among fans in St. Louis when Hornsby was traded to the New York Giants for Frankie Frisch in December 1926. Hornsby's .359 career average remains second only to Ty Cobb all-time.

In the previous century, the American Association's Browns featured some very effective hitters as well. Outfielder Tip O'Neill led the association in batting average in 1887 and 1888; his .435 mark in 1887 is the all-time franchise record and second-highest in major league history. A decade later, Jesse Burkett flirted with .400 but fell short, to .396, which was not even good enough to lead the National League. Burkett did win a batting crown in 1901 with a .376 mark.

Rogers Hornsby's Cardinals teams of the 1920s were by no means a one-man show. Jim Bottomley was often overshadowed by his larger-than-life teammate, but "Sunny Jim" batted over .300 in all but two seasons in St. Louis, with marks of .296 and .299 in his "off" years. He ranks ninth on the franchise all-time hit list. Another dangerous hitting teammate of Bottomley's during this period was outfielder Chick Hafey, who posted a .326 average in his eight years as a Cardinal, including a league-best and career-high mark of .349 in 1931. He was traded to Cincinnati after the 1931 season.

James "Tip" O'Neill, W.S. Kimball & Company cigarettes baseball card, 1888

Rogers Hornsby, circa 1922

Jim Bottomley, circa 1923

Joe Medwick, circa 1935

Stan Musial showing his batting pose, circa 1954

The Gas House Gang teams of the 1930s produced their own effective blend of speed and power in the offensive game. Joe Medwick was often chastised for swinging at balls outside the strike zone, but he connected often enough to secure the Triple Crown in 1937, making him the last National Leaguer to accomplish the feat. That year, he and teammate Johnny Mize engaged in a heated battle for the batting title, with Medwick's .374 edging out Mize's .363 mark. Three years earlier in 1934, when the Gas House Gang won its lone World Series, Medwick amazingly did not finish among the top-20 vote getters for the National League MVP Award, despite finishing in the top 10 in nearly every major statistical category. Some attributed the snub to Medwick's cold personality, which may have put off the writers. (Teammates Dizzy Dean, Paul Dean, Ripper Collins, and Frankie Frisch all received more votes than Medwick, with the award going to Dizzy Dean.)

Vying with Hornsby for the title of greatest all-time Cardinals hitter is the man from Donora, Pennsylvania, whose batting stance looked like he was peeking around the corner. Young Stan Musial originally came to the St. Louis organization as a pitcher, but after he injured his left (throwing) arm while stumbling over the sprinkler system in Orlando's Tinker Field, Musial decided to make a go of it as a position player instead. Several Cardinals scouts and minor league coaches chastised Musial's poor form at the plate, but Branch Rickey told them to leave him alone. "He hits the ball hard," Rickey simply pointed out in 1940. "Let him be." The result over the next 22 years was a (then) National League record of 3,630 hits—including an equal amount of 1,815 in Sportsman's Park and on the road. He was so feared in Brooklyn's home stadium of Ebbets Field that many in the stands would tremble when Musial approached the plate. "Here comes that man," they would whimper, and the nickname was ultimately extended to "Stan the Man" to designate the most beloved St. Louis player of all time. Paralleled with his hitting dominance was the way he endeared himself to fans with his simplicity and down-to-earth charm, exemplified by his willingness to bring out his harmonica and produce a tune on a moment's notice. A .331 career hitter, Musial nabbed seven batting titles, was named to the all-star team in every season from 1943 to 1963 (except when he was in the military in 1945), and won the National League MVP Award in 1943, 1946, and 1948. He spent his entire career with the

Cardinals and is the all-time franchise leader in games, at bats, hits, runs, doubles, triples, home runs, RBI, and walks.

The numerous Cardinals hitting marks established by Musial, however, may be met or eclipsed by the latest Redbirds slugger, Albert Pujols. In 2008, Pujols extended his own record in being the only player ever to hit 30 home runs, drive in more than 100 runs, and bat over .300 in each of his first eight major league seasons. His .334 career average (through 2008) is the highest among active players, and in 2003 he won a batting title with a .359 mark. He was named Rookie of the Year in 2001 and has finished at least fourth in the MVP Award voting every year except one since entering the league, winning the honors in 2005.

Albert Pujols

Second Basemen

With a history that has largely trumpeted speed, pitching, and defense in establishing success, it is ironic that the Cardinals have often enjoyed an extra batting boost from an unlikely source—the second base position. A spot often reserved for players that provide steady glove work but limited batting capability, Cardinals second baseman have frequently proven to be valuable offensive commodities.

The traditional role of second basemen offering little in the way of hitting prowess was clearly exemplified in the team's early years, when the four-time pennant-winning Browns featured a career .241 hitter at the keystone position, Yank Robinson. Possessing a good eye at the plate, however, Robinson was able to draw numerous bases on balls, and he led the league with a .400 on-base percentage despite batting only .231 in 1888.

Yank Robinson, Old Judge cigarettes baseball card, 1888

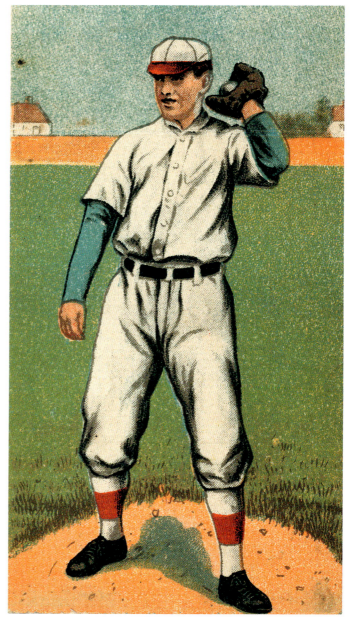

Miller Huggins, Mecca cigarettes baseball card, 1911

Rogers Hornsby, circa 1925

Miller Huggins played second base for the Cardinals from 1910 to 1915, and he too was effective at earning free passes, not so much at earning base hits. He led the league in walks in 1910 and 1914 before moving on to make a name for himself as a manager.

The man who broke the mold of the light-hitting second baseman in St. Louis, and in the league at large, is no less than one of the greatest hitters in the game's history, Rogers Hornsby. (His achievements are discussed in the preceding chapter on "Hit Men.") When the "Rajah" was dealt to New York in 1926, he was swapped for another future Hall of Famer in Frankie Frisch. Frisch quickly proved his own star value by winning the MVP Award in 1931 before being named player-manager of the Cards in 1933. Statistically, Frisch's best season was probably 1930, when he batted .346 and drove in a career-best 114 runs, although those numbers are dwarfed by league-wide statistical inflation during that hitter-friendly season. A threat on the base paths as well as at the plate, Frisch stole 48 bases in 1927 to lead the league. He was also a great bunter and rarely struck out, displaying the fundamental skills that make for an effective teaching model for a manager.

Following the trail blazed by Hornsby and Frisch was a series of short-timers at second base until the arrival of a local hero in the late 1940s. A native of nearby Germantown, Illinois, Red Schoendienst set a new standard at the position over more than a decade. He

Frankie Frisch forcing out Jimmie Foxx at second base, 1931 World Series

Julian Javier turning a double play against the New York Yankees, 1964 World Series

Red Schoendienst turning a double play over Boston's Johnny Pesky, 1946 World Series

debuted in 1945 as an outfielder but moved to second base for the 1946 championship season. That year he earned the first of what would be nine all-star selections as a Cardinal between 1946 and 1955. Although he had a .289 career average and finished second in the league with a .342 mark in 1953, it was his near-flawlessness with the glove that set Schoendienst apart. In 1953, he handled a then–National League record 320 consecutive chances at second base without an error. In a heartbreaking trade, Schoendienst was sent to the New York Giants in 1956 (and later, the Milwaukee Braves) before returning home to the Cardinals in 1961. Elected to the National Baseball Hall of Fame in 1989, Schoendienst remains active within the Cardinals organization more than 60 years after first joining the team as a 22-year-old rookie.

The next steady presence at the position for the Cardinals would actually play *for* Schoendienst when the latter became the field manager in 1965. Julian Javier never quite attained the offensive prowess (a .257 career mark) that his skipper achieved, but he quickly showed his skills as one of the greatest pursuers of pop flies the game had ever seen at the second base position. Javier was part of three pennant winners during his career with the Cardinals (1960–1971), adding to the club's attack as an adept bunter and surprising clutch hitter.

While Ted Sizemore and Mike Tyson provided solid play throughout the 1970s, another true turning point of the Cardinals in the 1980s was the emergence of Tommy Herr at second base, made possible by the move of Ken Oberkfell over to third base in 1981. In taking his place among the great running St. Louis teams of the decade, Herr did considerable damage with his bat as well, exemplified in 1985, when he drove in 110 runs despite knocking only eight homers. That season he also posted career high in hits (180), runs (97), doubles (38), walks (80), and stolen bases (31) to earn the only all-star selection of his 13-year career.

One of Herr's heirs at the position was Jose Oquendo, who had arrived from the New York Mets in 1985 and served as a backup infielder and outfielder before earning the starting second base job in 1989. He shared time with Luis Alicea over the next several years, contributing when and where he was needed. Oquendo continues to be a respected member of the Cardinals as the team's third base coach.

During the late 1990s and into the new century, the St. Louis tradition of speedy, offensive-minded players at second base continued with Delino Deshields, Fernando Viña, Adam Kennedy, and others. Tony Womack manned the keystone position during the 2004 pennant season, batting .307 and stealing 26 bases in his brief turn in St. Louis. Aaron Miles was an effective utility man in 2008, spending most of his time at second base while contributing a .317 average.

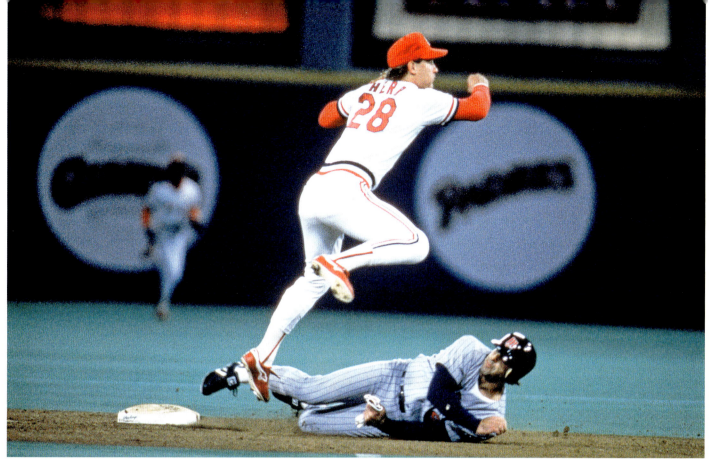

Tommy Herr turning a double play against the Minnesota Twins, 1987 World Series

Fernando Vina turning a double play against the Arizona Diamondbacks

Aaron Miles, 2008

Shortstops

It is difficult to field a winning baseball club—at any level—without strong defensive play up the middle. In addition to a steady second baseman, a reliable shortstop is a must, and the Cardinals have been blessed with some of the finest to ever man the position.

Perhaps the exception that proves the rule, the St. Louis Browns won three straight American Association pennants from 1885 to 1887 despite having a shortstop, Bill Gleason, who committed 535 errors in 796 career games at the position. (For comparison's sake, Ozzie Smith made 281 errors in 2,511 games.)

The pennant winners of the late 1920s and early 1930s also lacked shortstops with major star quality, but they did their part with solid contributions. Tommy Thevenow hit .417 against the Yankees in the 1926 World Series after batting just .256 during the regular season. Charlie Gelbert was the starting shortstop from 1929 to 1932 and chipped in a .304 average in 1930.

The 1934 Gas House Gang featured at shortstop a scrappy spark plug for whom winning was the utmost priority. "If I was over playing third base," Leo Durocher once said, "and my mother was rounding third with the winning run, I'd trip her. Oh, I'd pick her up, dust her off and say, 'Sorry Mom,' but nobody beats *me*."

Such was the fighting spirit that characterized the captain of the Gas House Gang—a player who was so skilled defensively that he remained in Frankie Frisch's lineup on a regular basis, despite the fact that none other than Babe Ruth had earlier nicknamed Durocher "The All-American Out" due to his ineptness as a hitter. Durocher enjoyed running with the high-society crowd when away from the ballpark, claiming Dean Martin and other celebrities among his close personal friends. Later in life, the media marveled at how Durocher's debonair ways off the field contrasted with the grit he displayed between the baselines. "Leo's 60, he looks 50, and acts 40," penned one Chicago writer after Durocher became the Cubs manager.

Durocher's form at shortstop, though highly effective, was typical of the choppy mechanics and two-handed defensive play of

Bill Gleason, Gold Coin Chewing Tobacco baseball card, 1887

Leo Durocher practicing his glove work during spring training, 1937

Marty Marion turning a double play against the Brooklyn Dodgers, October 1946

the era. Later, after Durocher had moved on to Brooklyn to become player-manager of the Dodgers, the smoother and silkier Marty Marion took over at short for the Cardinals. The 6-foot-2 Marion proved that a taller man could effectively play the position. He displayed as wide a range as anyone had seen in the game, paving the way for future tall shortstops such as Don Kessinger, Dick Groat, and Cal Ripken Jr. Despite batting only .267 in 1944, Marion earned the National League MVP Award for his slick fielding and everyday reliability amidst the war-depleted major league rosters.

Groat was a nine-year veteran and a former MVP with the Pirates by the time he came to the Cardinals in 1963. After batting .319 and collecting 201 hits in his first season in St. Louis, he was a valuable asset in the Cards' 1964 pennant charge. By 1966, Groat had given way to youngster Dal Maxvill at shortstop. Maxvill was a native of Granite City, Illinois, a town famous for its steel mills and located just across the river and ten miles north of St. Louis. While Maxvill struggled to post a .217 career batting average, his spectacular glove work assured him a place in the big leagues for 14 seasons. He also had a front-office career with several clubs after his playing days were over.

Dal Maxvill turning a double play against the Detroit Tigers, 1968 World Series

Garry Templeton broke in as the Cardinals' full-time starting shortstop in 1977 and put up impressive numbers in his rookie campaign (.322, 200 hits, 18 triples, 79 RBI, .449 slugging). He went on to bat over .300 three more times by 1981 and used his speed to lead the league in triples in each of his first three major league seasons. The main contribution of the two-time all-star, however, was as trade bait in what would be the coup de grace of Whitey Herzog's era of wheeling and dealing. When Herzog shipped Templeton to San Diego after the 1981 season in exchange for Ozzie Smith, he changed St. Louis' fortunes for years to come.

No one at the position had shown a greater combination of range and athleticism than Smith, who provided Cardinals pitchers with a sure out on ground balls to the left side of the field. The 15-time all-star hung his Hall of Fame credentials on his superior fielding—which garnered 13 consecutive Gold Glove Awards from 1980 through 1992—but the "Wizard of Oz" did contribute on offense as well. An adept bunter and stolen-base threat, Smith won a Silver Slugger Award in 1987 as the league's best hitting shortstop, and his dramatic

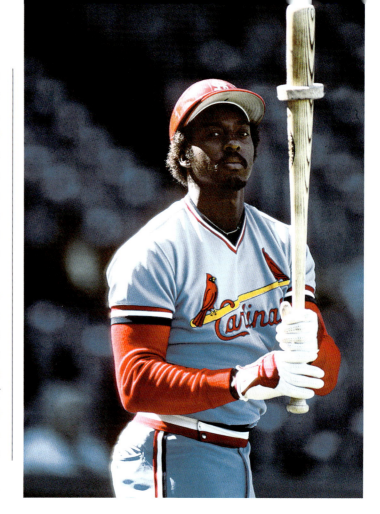

Garry Templeton, 1981

Ozzie Smith turning a double play against the Kansas City Royals, 1985 World Series

Edgar Renteria turning a double play against the Philadelphia Phillies, April 2004

David Eckstein turning a double play against the Pittsburgh Pirates, April 2007

walk-off home run against the Dodgers in the 1985 National League Championship Series helped catapult the Cardinals to the World Series. (It was also the first-ever left-handed homer by the switch-hitting Smith.)

As he entered the waning years of his career, the 41-year-old Smith graciously split time with his heir-apparent, Royce Clayton, in 1996. Clayton earned a trip to the All-Star Game in 1997 but was traded to Texas midway through the 1998 season.

Shortstops with great range and hands but average arms was the general rule with the Cardinals—including Durocher, Maxvill, Smith, and others—an exception being the short stint of former Chicago Cub Shawon Dunston and his rocket shots across the diamond in 1999 and 2000. Dunston was used at third base and in the outfield for much of his time in St. Louis as Edgar Renteria got the call at shortstop from 1999 to 2004. Renteria brought speed and decent home run power to the position while also winning Gold Gloves in 2002 and 2003. He made the all-star team three times and won three Silver Slugger awards during his six seasons in St. Louis.

Reviving the status quo of the light-hitting, mechanical-fielding shortstop was David Eckstein, who came to St. Louis from the Anaheim Angels in 2005. The 5-foot-6 Eckstein never permitted his physical limitations to impede his team's success, as he landed spots in the All-Star Game in his first two years in a Cardinals uniform and was named World Series MVP in 2006, batting .364 in the club's victory over the Detroit Tigers.

Third Basemen

One could argue that the position that produced the most "tough guys" in Cardinals history is third base. One individual in particular stands out in this regard, in the midst of America's toughest times.

"I don't care if they can field or not," a Cardinals scout in the 1930s once said of the kind of player he was seeking to play third base for the organization. "I want strong-armed, strong-chested men who can hit and run and throw. Guys like—well, like Pepper Martin."

Before Martin made the switch from the outfield to third base in the 1930s, the "hot corner" in St. Louis had been manned by a multitude of players, the most notable of whom goes all the way back to the franchise's origins in the old American Association. From 1883 to 1889, the spot was held by the fleet Arlie Latham, who recorded 739 stolen bases in his big league career. Even with all the legendary base runners in Cardinals history, Latham still holds the top single-season figure for the St. Louis franchise, with 129 steals for the Browns in 1887.

The franchise's first championship team of the twentieth century featured all-time great hitters like Rogers Hornsby and Jim Bottomley, but the highest batting average on that 1926 squad was produced by little-known third bagger Les Bell, at .325. He also led the way with a .518 slugging percentage, while only Bottomley did better than Bell's 17 homers and 100 RBI.

Whitey Kurowski immediately became a favorite in St. Louis when he clubbed his World Series–winning homer against the Yankees in 1942, his first year as a starter. He arrived on the team in time to provide some stability on a roster that would see many of its stars, including Enos Slaughter, Terry Moore, and eventually Stan Musial, depart for service in World War II. A five-time all-star, Kurowski spent his entire nine-year career with the Cardinals

Pepper Martin at spring training, circa 1934

Whitey Kurowski at spring training, 1942

before arm troubles brought his career to an end when he was just 31 years old.

Missouri native Ken Boyer formed a rock-solid post at third base for a decade (1955–1965) and earned the league MVP Award in 1964 while helping the Cards secure another World Series victory over the Yankees. Boyer hit more than 30 home runs in a season only once in his career, but his 255 home runs as a Cardinal trails only Musial and Pujols. The versatile Boyer also won five Gold Glove Awards.

Following closely in the mold of Pepper Martin was Mike Shannon, a native of south St. Louis who briefly pursued a football career as a quarterback at the University of Missouri. When Boyer was dealt away following the 1965 season, the team struggled to find a replacement. After home run slugger Roger Maris joined the Cardinals in 1967, Shannon was asked by manager Red Schoendienst to move from right field to third base, a position Shannon essentially had never played before—just as Martin had done for the Cardinals back in 1933. And just like Martin, Shannon played the position in an unorthodox but effective manner, using his strong upper body to knock the ball down and a strong arm to atone for needing extra time to grasp it—just as the old Cardinals scout had wanted to see it done. Shannon's career ended prematurely due to a kidney disorder when he was just 30 in 1970.

Ken Boyer at spring training, 1957

Mike Shannon batting during 1964 World Series

Joe Torre, 1971

Ken Oberkfell batting during 1982 World Series

Nineteen years before he would return to St. Louis as manager of the Cardinals, Joe Torre slammed his way to the National League MVP Award as the team's third baseman in 1971 by posting a .363 average, the highest by a Cardinal since Musial's .365 in 1946. As it was with Shannon and Martin, third base was not Torre's original position, but the former catcher and first baseman moved to third base to take over for Shannon. The emergence of Ken Reitz at the hot corner allowed Torre to move back to first in 1973. Reitz, "The Ol' Zamboni," had a magnificent glove but swung a mediocre bat and was proclaimed to be one of the slowest men in the major leagues.

The 1980s saw the emergence of a pair of versatile players who not only took their turns at third base for the Cardinals but assisted the club at other positions as well. Ken Oberkfell came out of nearby Highland, Illinois, to serve as a steadying influence at second base for the Redbirds but soon made the shift to third to make room for Tommy Herr. Similarly, the power-hitting Todd Zeile was touted as one of the game's top catching prospects in the late 1980s but spent only a year as the starter in that position. When Tom Pagnozzi took over behind the plate in 1991, Zeile took his talents down the line. In between the stints of Oberkfell and Zeile was Terry Pendleton, who helped

Scott Rolen, 2004

the Cards to two pennants during his six and half seasons as the team's third baseman.

The tradition of bringing in players with local connections continued with the acquisition of Gary Gaetti in 1996. A native of Centralia, Illinois (60 miles east of St. Louis), Gaetti spent 1996 and 1997 with the Cardinals before being released in August 1998. The void was filled by Dominican-born Fernando Tatis, who belted 34 homers in 1999 but is best known for hitting two grand slams in one inning, accomplished against the Dodgers in April of that season.

Scott Rolen, a southern Indiana native, was acquired in a trade with the Philadelphia Phillies in mid-2002. Rolen was an all-star in his first four full seasons in St. Louis, his best performance coming in the 2004 pennant year when he batted .314 and hit 34 home runs. Another slugging third baseman, Troy Glaus, arrived for the 2008 season to replace Rolen in the lineup, hopeful of adding his name among the top sluggers in team history.

Troy Glaus, 2008

Outfielders

Supreme fly ball chasers have been a hallmark of Cardinals baseball since the first deep one was lofted to the outer pastures of the original Sportsman's Park. Through most of the 1900s, the Cardinals utilized speed not only on the base paths but also on defense to counter the typical lumbering, power-laden teams from the eastern cities of the National League.

Long before the Cardinals were even known as the Cardinals, the St. Louis Browns of the mid to late 1880s wreaked havoc on the American Association. Along with infielders Charles Comiskey and Arlie Latham, outfielder James "Tip" O'Neill was integral to the team's success. His .435 batting average in 1887 ranks as the second-best in the history of big league baseball. Tommy McCarthy played alongside O'Neill for three seasons, and in 1890 (when O'Neill jumped to the renegade Players League), McCarthy blazed his way to a .350 average, 137 runs scored, and 83 stolen bases. The speed of O'Neill, McCarthy, and others in the outfield helped the St. Louis pitchers hold down the opposition.

As the Cardinals struggled to climb back to the top of the standings through the early part of the twentieth century, a few noteworthy players took their positions in the Sportman's Park outfield. Future Hall of Famer Jesse Burkett posted a scorching .378 average over his three seasons in St. Louis (1899–1901), while Patsy Donovan chipped in with a .314 mark from 1900 to 1903.

Taylor Douthit covered center field for the pennant-winning clubs of 1926, 1928, and 1930, but his spot was taken over by Pepper Martin beginning in 1931. After joining the team in 1924, Chick Hafey grew into a starting role by 1927 and launched a Hall of Fame career over the next five seasons. A .317 career hitter, Hafey led the National League with a .349 average in 1931 before being traded to Cincinnati.

A new collection of stars patrolled the outfield grass in subsequent decades. Slugger Joe Medwick covered the left field zone for most of the 1930s, while the fleet-footed Terry Moore roamed Sportsman's Park's vast center field from 1935 through

Tommy McCarthy, Old Judge cigarettes baseball card, circa 1887

Chick Hafey, 1926

1948, missing three years due to World War II. When Moore and right fielder Enos "Country" Slaughter would cross each other in the gap at Sportsman's, it happened so quickly that spectators and sportswriters often couldn't tell which one had caught the ball. Slaughter also missed three entire seasons (1943–1945) for service in World War II, but he didn't seem to miss a beat. After hitting .318 with 98 RBI and 100 runs scored in 1942, Slaughter returned in 1946 and posted a .300 average, 130 RBI, and another 100-run season, a mark he would repeat for a third time in 1947.

Slaughter, a 10-time all-star, and Moore, who earned four trips to the Midsummer Classic, were joined in 1942 by an outfielder who make 24 All-Star Game appearances during his career. Although not quite as quick afoot as his two outfield mates, Stan Musial found other ways to contribute to his team's success while still playing an above-average defensive game.

Stan Musial practicing his fielding, 1942

Below: *Enos Slaughter, Terry Moore, and Stan Musial, 1946*

As Musial flipped back and forth from the outfield to first base, a variety of players rotated in and out of the lineup during the 1950s. Wally Moon was the most notable addition to the outfield position. Named the National League Rookie of the Year in 1954, Moon remained with St. Louis through the 1958 season.

More stability returned to the Cardinals rosters in the 1960s, and this was particularly evident in the outfield. Beginning in 1958, Curt Flood spent 12 years as the team's center fielder, winning seven Gold Gloves in the process. He was joined by left fielder Lou Brock in mid-1964. While possessing great speed and consequently an ability to run down liners over a great distance, Brock never appeared fully comfortable as an outfielder. Mike Shannon played three seasons in right field before being shifted to third base to make room for the newly acquired Roger Maris in 1967. Although his best days were behind him, Maris helped St. Louis secure back-to-back pennants in his two seasons with the team.

After Brock finally gave up the left field job in 1979, he was ultimately replaced by a player who shared some of Brock's uneasiness in the field. Lonnie Smith, who was acquired from Philadelphia in 1982, secured the nickname of "Skates" from the uncertain manner in which he approached a ball batted in his direction, often making a routine play look theatrical. While not quite up to Brock's standards of base thievery, Smith was a dangerous threat on the base paths.

Arnold "Bake" McBride won the 1974 Rookie of the Year Award while covering center field at Busch Stadium, and after he was traded to Philadelphia in 1977, the Cardinals searched long and hard to find another center fielder who could go get 'em like Bake could. Five years later, Willie McGee quickly emerged as the regular man in the middle, and he—along with fellow rookie David Green—helped lead the Cards to a World Series victory over the Milwaukee Brewers with dazzling plays in the field.

Curt Flood making a leaping catch at the wall, Wrigley Field, 1962

Lou Brock making a leaping catch at the wall, Wrigley Field, 1969

Lonnie Smith making a running catch, 1982 World Series

Willie McGee making a leaping catch at the wall, spring training 1999

George Hendrick, 1982 World Series

While players like Brock, Flood, McBride, McGee, Smith, and others were cherished in St. Louis for their speed in the outfield and on the base paths, George Hendrick was there to provide power at the plate. The right fielder led the team in homers in every season from 1980 through 1983, with a high of 25 in 1980. He was traded to Pittsburgh after the 1984 season for pitcher John Tudor, who went on to win 21 games for the Cardinals in 1985.

When Lonnie Smith was dealt to Kansas City in 1985, the door was opened for Vince Coleman, who like Smith and Brock offered superior speed in the left field position but marginal defensive skills and a sub-par throwing arm (in accuracy, if not in strength). Even so, Coleman and McGee teamed up for part of the 1980s with right fielder Andy Van Slyke to compose one of the fastest and most effective outfields in baseball history. Flying over the artificial turf of Busch Stadium, the trio denied opponents' extra-base hits with their galloping catches in the gaps.

During the 1990s, center fielder Ray Lankford was a relatively consistent presence in the Cardinals' mercurial outfield that also featured the likes of Bernard Gilkey, Brian Jordan, and Ron Gant. All four of them offered both speed and power—Lankford twice hit more than 30 homers in a season and twice stole 40 or more bases—but individually and as a group, they

Jim Edmonds robbing another home run ball, 2004

were unable to generate the kind of success the team had enjoyed in the previous decade.

While each Cardinals center fielder seemed to surpass his predecessor in defensive marvels—from Douthit to Moore to Flood to McGee—perhaps none exceeded the exploits of Jim Edmonds, who arrived in St. Louis from the Anaheim Angels in 2000 and quickly became a fan favorite. By 2005, Edmonds had collected eight career Gold Glove Awards, partially the product of the many dazzling over-the-wall and back-to-the-plate catches he pulled off in ballparks around the country, proving himself as one of baseball's best center fielders of all time in the process. And he could do some damage with the bat, too. Edmonds twice belted 42 long balls in a season, and heading into the 2009 season, he is approaching the 400 mark in career home runs.

As the Cardinals close out the first decade of the 2000s, the outfield attack is spearheaded by two players who rose from being relative unknowns before breaking out in St. Louis. Skip Schumaker was a fifth-round pick of the Cardinals in 2001 who finally became a regular in 2008, and Ryan Ludwick earned an appearance in the 2008 All-Star Game after serving essentially as a reserve with two other organizations before joining the Cardinals prior to the 2007 season. Joining Schumaker and Ludwick in the outfield was Rick Ankiel, who re-energized his career after a total meltdown as a pitcher to assume Edmonds' position as the Cardinals center fielder for much of 2008.

Rick Ankiel (#24), Skip Schumaker (#55), and Ryan Ludwick (#47), 2008

Frankie Frisch sliding into third base, 1934 World Series

The Jackrabbits

Fleet-footed Redbirds and the Cardinals' overall running game have provided some of the most electric moments in baseball history. Sitting in the stands at Sportsman's Park or Busch Stadium, one can imbibe it; watching a game on television, one can see it; and listening to Harry Caray or Jack Buck describe it on the radio, one could feel it.

The assault was first launched by Arlie Latham's 129 stolen bases in 1887—still a franchise record—and the attack has for the most part been unrelenting. (Ironically, the 1949 Cardinals hold the record for the *fewest* stolen bases in a National League season with 17.) Charlie Comiskey nabbed 117 bases in that same 1887 season, and Latham and Tommy McCarthy stole 109 and 93 bases, respectively, in 1888.

The modern era of base-running legends for the Cardinals was furthered by Frankie Frisch and Pepper Martin during the late 1920s and early 1930s. Frisch twice led the league in stolen bases in an era when the home run was becoming baseball's main attraction. In an outstanding performance during the 1931

Pepper Martin stealing second base, 1934 World Series

World Series against the heavily favored Philadelphia A's, Martin raced circles around the A's and their immortal catcher Mickey Cochrane. He took daring chances on the base paths in a manner that would come to symbolize the team's aggressiveness in the decades to come. Martin was also the National League's regular-season stolen base king three times from 1933 to 1936.

Cardinals speed and aggressiveness on the base paths was on full display in the 1960s, primarily behind the jets of Curt Flood, Lou Brock, and Julian Javier. Their prowess on the bases led to three pennants that decade. Beginning in 1965, his first full season in St. Louis, Brock posted 12 straight seasons with at least 50 stolen bases. In 1974—the year he turned 35 years old—Brock showed that he had not lost a step, as he shattered Maury Wills' modern-era single-season record with 118 stolen bases. While Bake McBride, Garry Templeton, Tony Scott, and others added their speedy skills to Brock's in the 1970s, no era would match the St. Louis base-running production of the 1980s.

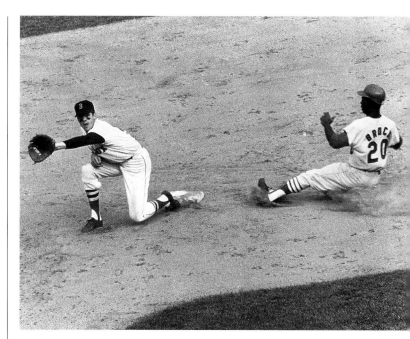
Lou Brock stealing second base, 1967 World Series

Willie McGee running the bases, 1983

The speed onslaught of the 1980s began with the emergence of Willie McGee, a rookie outfielder in 1982. McGee was originally a seventh-round draft pick of the Chicago White Sox in 1976, but after failing to sign with the Sox, he was taken in the first round by the New York Yankees a year later. He was traded to the Cardinals at the conclusion of the 1981 season and went on to be a central piece on St. Louis' pennant-winning teams of the decade. McGee used his speed not just to steal bases and score runs but also to win Gold Glove Awards in the outfield. He was the National League MVP and batting champion in 1985, despite starting the year with an injury. While McGee was laid up, a young outfielder was summoned from the Louisville farm team to fill in. General Manager Dal Maxvill made it clear to Vince Coleman that his current stay in the major leagues would be brief, lasting only until McGee could come off the disabled list. "Yes sir, Mr. Maxvill, I understand," Coleman replied, "but I'm going to be up here all year." Maxvill smiled in appreciation of the rookie's confidence but repeated his edict once again. Coleman, in turn, repeated his assertion that he expected to be on the St. Louis roster all summer—and ultimately, Maxvill and Herzog could not disagree. Coleman, a regular stolen base champ in the minor leagues, finished his rookie year with an amazing 110 steals, a record for a first-year player. Coleman's total accounted for over a third of the 314 bases that the Cards swiped in 1985—the most in the National League in nearly one hundred years and the yardstick by which great St. Louis running teams have since been measured. The outfield trio of Coleman, McGee, and Van Slyke alone stole 200 bases among them. Coleman went on to lead the league in thefts in every season that he played for the Cardinals (1985–1990).

Though unable to stay healthy for most of his time in St. Louis, outfielder Brian Jordan excited fans with his long-striding gallops around the bases in Busch Stadium during the 1990s. The former professional football player often worked with expert track coaches to maximize his sprinting speed, and it paid off for the Cardinals on both offense and defense. The Cardinals of the late 2000s did not feature one dominant stolen base artist as had teams of the past but did provide multiple moderate threats throughout the lineup.

Vince Coleman running the bases, 1990

Brian Jordan running the bases, 1998

The Home Run Kings

Although the team has mostly played in spacious ballparks with an offense centered around speed over power, the Cardinals have had their share of notable home run hitters.

Going back to the dead-ball era of the nineteenth century, outfielder Oscar Walker led the American Association with seven homers in the Browns' inaugural season of 1882, and Tip O'Neill belted a league-high 14 to go along with his .435 batting average in 1887. As a team, St. Louis led the league in home runs every season from 1886 through 1891.

After baseball entered the "lively ball" era in 1920, the Redbirds' first home run king was Rogers Hornsby, who knocked 42 in 1922 and then 39 in 1925. "Sunny Jim" Bottomley tied Chicago's Hack Wilson for the league lead in 1928 with 31, and Joe Medwick knotted Mel Ott of the Giants atop the league with the same total in 1937.

An unheralded star from the Gas House Gang, James "Ripper" Collins led the National League in home runs (35) and slugging percentage (.615) during the 1934 championship season. Medwick was joined by Johnny Mize as the team's main sluggers in the 1930s. Mize won back-to-back crowns in 1939 and 1940, and his 43 dingers in 1940 stood as the franchise single-season mark until the arrival of Mark McGwire more than half a century later.

The all-time home run leader for the St. Louis Cardinals never once led the league in that category. Stan Musial was among the top ten home run hitters 12 times in his 22-year-career, but the closest he got to number one was when he hit 39 to Mize and Ralph Kiner's 40 in 1948. Still, with six seasons of 30 or more homers, Stan the Man's 475 career home runs currently rank him twenty-eighth on the all-time home run list.

Ken Boyer spent a decade with St. Louis and trails only Musial and Albert Pujols on the franchise leader board, but his single-season home run high was 32 in 1960—fourth best in the National League. George Hendrick hit a few long balls

Johnny Mize, 1936

Stan Musial, 1962

Jack Clark, 1985

Mark McGwire hitting home run number 62, 1998

for the Cardinals of the early 1980s, but Jack Clark was the team's only true power hitter of the decade. He peaked in 1987 with 35 homers while leading the league in slugging percentage.

The arrival of Mark McGwire in 1997 brought a sudden and dramatic power surge to St. Louis. In his four-and-a-half seasons with the team, Big Mac belted 220 home runs, leading baseball with astonishing totals of 70 and 65 in 1998 and 1999, respectively.

Albert Pujols took the slugger's baton from McGwire in 2001, and although he has not yet led the league in homers, Pujols is the only player in major league history to begin his career with eight straight seasons of 30 or more home runs (through 2008). His career-high total of 49 in 2006 placed him second in the circuit behind Ryan Howard (58) of the Philadelphia Phillies.

Albert Pujols, 2008

Starting Pitchers

While much attention has been given to the offensive prowess of Cardinals teams over the years, the men taking the mound for St. Louis have etched their own colorful and successful history as well. The Cardinals have been privileged to hold some of the greatest starting pitchers the game has seen, and as with most clubs before the 1970s, the Cards would permit their starters to venture deep into their assignments—and the heavy workload was welcomed.

"The only reason I entered the army," Dizzy Dean would later say, "was so that I could eat and pitch every day." To be certain, Dean was emblematic of days long-gone by, when managers would send their best pitchers out to the mound every fourth day (instead of every fifth day, as is the norm today) and when the relegation of a pitcher to the bullpen was truly a banishment, summoned into action only in the instance of a lopsided game. Dean always complained to manager Frankie Frisch about "not gettin' to pitch 'nuff," even though arm injuries would bring his career to a premature end. Still, Dean's performance from 1932 to 1936 was as dominant as any five-year run by any pitcher in history. During that span, he led the National League in wins twice, strikeouts four times, and complete games three times while averaging 24 wins and 194 strikeouts. In 1934, when he won the league MVP Award, Dean became the last National League hurler to win 30 games in a season. (Six years after retiring as a pitcher for the Cubs at the age of 31, Dean returned to pitch one game for the Browns in 1947. After he chastised the Browns' pitching staff over the radio and incurred the wrath of the wives of the Browns' pitchers, he took them up on their suggestion that Dean go out to the mound and see if he could do better.) Dean was enshrined in the Baseball Hall of Fame in 1953.

Nearly half a century before Dean won his last major league game, the St. Louis Browns organization had six different pitchers win 30 or more games in season during the 1880s and 1890s. From 1887 to 1889, Charles "Silver" King *averaged* 37 wins per year, with a franchise-record 45 wins in 1888. King also had a 1.64 ERA while completing 64 of the 65 games he started.

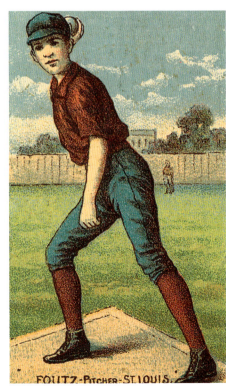

Dave Foutz, Gold Coin Chewing Tobacco baseball card, 1887

Slim Sallee warming up, 1913

Cardinals pitchers before the 1930 World Series, including Bill Hallahan (far left), Jesse Haines (fourth from right), and Burleigh Grimes (far right)

Two years earlier, Dave Foutz posted a 41–16 record with 11 shutouts, and Foutz's teammate Bob Caruthers won 99 games between 1885 and 1887.

During the 1910s, when the Cardinals weren't winning a lot of games, Slim Sallee managed to earn 15 or more victories in four consecutive seasons. In 1920, "Spittin' Bill" Doak had a record of 20–12 (.625) while the team went 75–79 (.487).

Whereas Doak and the top hurlers of the 1880s and 1890s were all right handed, Bill Sherdel became the first Cardinals southpaw in the twentieth century to win 20 games in a season when he went 21–10 in St. Louis' pennant campaign of 1928. That year, righty Jesse Haines posted his third 20-win season of the decade, and future Hall of Famer Grover Cleveland "Pete" Alexander, at age 41, chipped in with 16 victories. Haines was also one of six Cardinals starters to win at least 11 games in 1931; lefty "Wild Bill" Hallahan led the way with 19 wins, and Hall of Famer Burleigh Grimes added 17.

Dizzy Dean, circa 1936

Above: *Cardinals pitchers before the 1943 World Series (left to right): Mort Cooper, Ernie White, Max Lanier, Al Brazle*

Left: *Harry Brecheen, circa 1947*

The Cardinals teams that captured four pennants and three world championships during the 1940s did not boast any hurlers who would be enshrined in Cooperstown, but they got plenty of support and hard work from the likes of Mort Cooper, Max Lanier, Harry Brecheen, and others. Cooper won the National League MVP Award in 1942 with 22 wins, a 1.78 ERA, and 10 shutouts, all league highs. He followed that with 21 wins in 1943 and 22 again in 1944 while losing a total of 22 games over the three seasons (1942–1944). Brecheen won at least 15 games in every season from 1944 through 1948, peaking with 20 in 1948.

Though some three decades separated their careers, the endurance, confidence, and overpowering fastball displayed by Bob Gibson in the 1960s compare to what Dizzy Dean was doing in the 1930s. Gibson made his major league debut in 1959 and truly began his rise as an elite pitcher in 1962 when he struck out 208 batters in 234 innings and led the league with 5 shutouts. Two years later, Gibson notched 19 regular-season wins to help the Cardinals capture the pennant, and

Bob Gibson, circa 1968

then he added two crucial victories over the Yankees in the World Series. Except for the injury-shortened 1967 campaign, he won at least 20 games every year from 1965 to 1970. During his extraordinary 1968 season, Gibson completed 28 of the 34 games he started and was removed for a pinch hitter in the six contests he didn't complete. This was part of a streak from mid-1967 to mid-1969 during which Gibson was not removed from a game in the midst of a defensive inning. However, stamina was possibly the least impressive of Gibson's accomplishments in 1968. He posted the fourth-lowest qualifying earned run average in history (and the lowest in the post-dead-ball era) with a mark of 1.12, permitting just 198 hits while striking out 268 in 305 innings of work. He threw 13 shutouts and finished with a 22–9 record. The performance earned him the Cy Young and MVP Awards, and he added another Cy Young trophy in 1970. The versatile and athletic Gibson also won nine consecutive Gold Glove Awards (1965–1973) and could handle the bat well for a pitcher. He entered the Hall of Fame in 1981 with a career total of 3,117 strikeouts and 251 wins, both Cardinals franchise records.

Another future Hall of Famer joined Gibson in the rotation from 1967 to 1971, although Steve "Lefty" Carlton mostly made his name while pitching for the Phillies from 1972 through 1986. As a Cardinal, Carlton went 77–62, winning 20 games in 1971 and finishing second in the league with a 2.17 ERA in 1969.

Steve Carlton pitching during the All-Star Game, July 1969

Bob Forsch pitching a no-hitter, April 16, 1978

Joaquin Andujar, 1982

John Tudor, 1985

The post-Gibson era began with the 1976 season, and the result for the remainder of the decade was an up-and-down pitching staff in St. Louis. The main exception was the emergence of Bob Forsch as a top-flight starter. Forsch built a reputation as a solid hitter after being drafted by the Cards as a shortstop in 1968, but the club soon found that his throwing arm was best suited for the hill. Joining older brother Ken (a member of the Houston Astros and California Angels) as a big league pitcher, Forsch started 14 games as a rookie for St. Louis in 1974 and spent parts of the next 15 seasons with the team. He is the only Cardinals pitcher to hurl two no-hitters, one on April 16, 1978, against Philadelphia and the other on September 26, 1983, against Montreal.

Along with his individual accolades, Forsch was an integral part of an imposing starting staff during the 1980s that included Joaquin Andujar, John Tudor, and others. Tudor's 1.93 ERA in 1985 is the lowest by a Cardinals pitcher since Gibson's incredible 1968 number. Tudor and Andujar each won 21 games during the 1985 pennant season.

The 1990s produced neither pennants nor superstar pitchers in St. Louis (Bob Tewksbury was the team's winningest pitcher of the decade, with 66), but in 2005, Chris Carpenter joined Gibson as the only Cardinals pitchers to win a Cy Young Award. Although he only led the league in one category (complete games), Carpenter's 21–5 record, 2.83 ERA, and 213 strikeouts put him in rare company. The Cardinals had high hopes for a dynamic duo when they acquired lefty Mark Mulder from Oakland in December 2004 season and later signed him in a multimillion-dollar deal, but after a 16–8 campaign in 2005, injuries short-circuited Mulder's career. He appeared in a total of six games in 2007 and 2008, posting an ERA of 12.05.

While Mulder was a disappointment, the Cards got a pleasant surprise from free agent acquisition Kyle Lohse. After mounting a record of 63–74 in his first seven seasons, Lohse bounced back with a 15–6 record and career-best 3.78 ERA in 2008. The team re-signed him to a four-year, $41-million contract following the season.

Chris Carpenter, 2005

Kyle Lohse, 2008

RELIEVERS

With workhorse starters such as Dizzy Dean, Bob Gibson, and others throughout the team's history, the Cardinals were perhaps slower than other franchises to adopt the modern use of the bullpen. Typically, in the early years of the organization, a relief pitcher was simply somebody who wasn't good enough to start or was called in on occasion to bail out a struggling starter. Nonetheless, the Redbirds have produced several notable relievers and notable late-game pitching moments, the first of which involved a most unlikely hero.

Grover Cleveland Alexander, circa 1926

The 1926 season was Grover Cleveland Alexander's first in a Cardinals uniform. He made his mark immediately and secured complete-game victories for the Redbirds in Games Two and Six of the World Series against the Yankees. Figuring his duties for the series were finished, he arrived at Game Seven admittedly still a little drunk from some late carousing the night before. When he was called out of the bullpen to relieve Jesse Haines in the seventh inning, Alexander got it together enough to pitch hitless ball the rest of the way and save the clinching game for St. Louis. Haines would himself become a key relief pitcher for the Cardinals later in his career.

Although the highly choreographed strategy of sending in left-handed pitchers to face left-handed batters and right-handed pitchers to face right-handed batters was still decades away, Cardinals manager Eddie Dyer had good options from both sides in his bullpen during the late 1940s. Righty Ted Wilks broke into the major leagues as a starter in 1944, but by 1946 he was making only a handful of starts. From that season until he was traded to Pittsburgh in June 1951, Wilks appeared in 228 games for St. Louis but started only 6 of them. Lefty Al Brazle, who spent his entire 10-year career with the Cards, joined the team as an occasional starter in 1943, and after a 2-year absence for World War II, Brazle was used primarily in a relief role upon his return in 1946. In 1952, he led the league and set a new team record with 16 saves and then improved on that in 1953, recording 18 saves while appearing in 60 games, all in relief.

By the end of the decade, Lindy McDaniel was perfecting the role of the relief specialist. His 26 saves in 1960 would not be matched by another Cardinals pitcher for more than two decades. During that all-star season, McDaniel appeared in 65 games while accumulating fewer than 117 innings pitched, meaning that he averaged less than two innings per appearance and thus presaged the short-relief strategy of later decades.

A variety of pitchers assumed the closer's role following McDaniel's departure in 1963, including Joe Hoerner, who did not start a single game in his 14-year career and was St. Louis' top saves man from 1966 to 1969. In the 1970s, however, the team featured one of the most effective—and most entertaining—relief pitchers of that era.

Jesse Haines, 1936

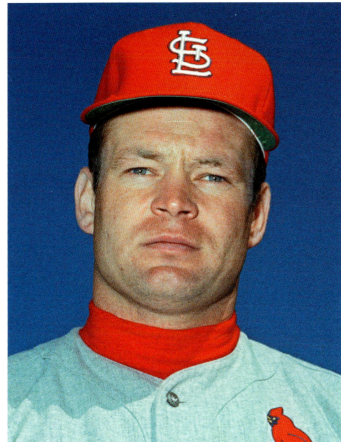
Joe Hoerner, 1968

Al Hrabosky, 1977

Bruce Sutter, 1982 World Series

Little left-hander Al Hrabosky was barely able to make his high school team but eventually worked his way onto a college roster, where he was noticed by scouts for the Cardinals. He was the club's first-round draft pick in 1969, and he made his big-league debut the next season. Known as "The Mad Hungarian," Hrabosky would work himself into a frenzy behind the pitcher's mound before every inning, and he used that competitive fire to become one of the game's dominant relievers. He led the National League in saves in 1975 while posting a record of 13–3, good enough for a third-place finish in the Cy Young Award voting.

After the 1977 season, the Cardinals swapped closers with the Kansas City Royals and received Mark Littell in exchange for Hrabosky. Littell, however, proved to be only a temporary solution, as the acquisition of Bruce Sutter from the Chicago Cubs in 1981 gave the team a future Hall of Famer in the bullpen. Sutter had exploded on the scene in 1976 with the Cubs, displaying his innovative split-fingered fastball, which produced a dramatic dropping effect when the ball reached home plate. He led the league with 25 saves in his first year with the Cardinals and repeated as saves champ with a mark of 36 in 1982. After recording the last out in the 1982 World Series, Sutter spent two

Todd Worrell, 1985 World Series

Jason Isringhausen, 2007

more years in a St. Louis uniform—and set a new National League record with 45 saves in 1984—before accepting a more lucrative contract with the Atlanta Braves before the 1985 season. Seemingly destined for failure with Sutter's departure, the Cardinals bullpen convalesced behind the group effort of Rick Horton, Jeff Lahti, Ken Dayley, and others to help produce a pennant in 1985.

Todd Worrell was a late-season call up in 1985 and contributed 3 wins and 5 saves during the stretch run. The next season, he was entrusted with the closer's role, and he met the challenge with 36 saves and a 2.08 ERA while winning the National League Rookie of the Year Award. A severe elbow injury late in 1989 forced Worrell to miss the entirety of the 1990 and 1991 seasons. (He would regain his all-star form with the Dodgers later in the decade.) The Cardinals went looking for somebody to take Worrell's place, and a trade with the Red Sox in May 1990 netted a Hall of Fame reliever in Lee Smith. Over the next three seasons, Smith saved 133 games for the Cardinals, setting a franchise record with 47 in 1991.

After growing up near Piasa, Illinois (just over the river from St. Louis), Jason Isringhausen became part of a highly regarded group of young New York Mets starting pitchers in the mid- and late-1990s that included Bobby Jones, Bill Pulsipher, and Paul Wilson. Wrought with a variety of injuries to each man, the group soon disbanded without reaching its potential. Isringhausen found his way home to St. Louis in 2002, and two years later he matched the single-season team record of 47 saves. By 2006, just his fifth year with the club, he held the organization's all-time saves mark, a number that totaled 217 through the 2008 season.

THE NAME GAME

The vibrant history of the Cardinals franchise is tied, in part, to the colorful nicknames that have been held by many of its players. The ace pitcher on the inaugural Brown Stockings team of 1882 was given the name George Washington McGinnis by his parents, but he was known as Jumbo McGinnis by his teammates. Jumbo's catcher, Thomas Jefferson Sullivan, was more commonly known as Sleeper Sullivan, or "Old Iron Hands." Later in the decade, the Browns won pennants with guys who went by Doc (Bushong), Yank (Robinson), Tip (O'Neill), and Silver (King). The 5-foot-6 Shorty Fuller played shortstop from 1889 to 1891; for part of the 1890 season he played alongside third baseman Jumbo Davis. While the nicknames may be memorable—and we haven't even mentioned Jocko, Duke, Dusty, Doggie, Kid, Dad, Count, Chief, and Toad, among others, who appeared in a Browns uniform—the players of the 1880s and 1890s are largely forgotten.

Later, in the 1920s, infielder George Toporczer gained the moniker "Specs" due to the thick eyeglasses he wore. Toporczer needed the glasses to correct the serious vision deformity that he had since birth, and which he did not allow to get in the way of his baseball career. Toporczer was a great contact hitter who struck out only 93 times in more than 1,500 major league at-bats. He later went completely blind, long before his death in 1989 at the age of 90.

Despite the different dates and places he gave writers to provide them their scoops, Jay Hanna Dean is widely accepted to have been born with that name on January 16, 1910, in Lucas, Arkansas. Dean, however, ultimately insisted that he changed his name to *Jerome Herman* Dean to honor a childhood friend who had died. Shortly after Dean lied about his age and entered the army at the age of 17, his drill sergeant caught him hurling freshly peeled potatoes at a garbage can one summer day. While his superiors deeply disapproved, Dean's fellow enlisted men were impressed by the strength and accuracy of his throwing arm. "You dizzy son of a ____!" hollered Army Sergeant James Brought—and the private's new nickname was soon circulating throughout the camp. The nickname would stick, and when Dean's brother Paul entered the big leagues two years after Dizzy, the writers forced the nickname "Daffy" on him for simple alliterative purposes. The other nickname for the younger, quiet Dean brother was more fitting: "Harpo," taken from the Marx brother who mostly stood mute and let the other brothers do the talking.

Catching the Dean boys for St. Louis from 1934 to 1936 was Virgil Davis. Because of his physical resemblance to the tubers that Dizzy had been known to fire around the army base, Davis was bestowed with the nickname of "Spud." Manning the third base position for this squad was Johnny Martin, nicknamed "The Wild Horse of the Osage" for his unpredictable behavior off the field. Martin's passion for juggling games with a baseball, however, earned him the snappier pseudonym of "Pepper" early in his career. Martin would magically flip a ball behind his back, over his head, between his legs, and a multitude of other ways in a session of acrobatic toss with his mates, much to the delight of the fans. Other colorfully nicknamed members of the Gas House

George "Specs" Toporczer, 1922

Jay Hanna "Dizzy" Dean and Paul "Daffy" Dean

Virgil "Spud" Davis

John "Pepper" Martin, at "Pepper Martin Day," June 1939

Gang included Joe "Ducky" Medwick, so named (much to his chagrin) for the slight waddle in his walk, and fellow slugger Johnny Mize, who earned the "Big Cat" moniker for his smooth moves in the field.

Men called Creepy, Country, and Whitey were main ingredients in the great Cardinals teams of the 1940s. Second baseman Frank "Creepy" Crespi had natural dark circles underneath his eyes, which inspired his unique nickname. A backup for his first three years on the roster, Crespi earned the starting second baseman role in 1941, his only full season as a regular. In 1943, he broke his leg during a serviceman's game while in the army during World War II, and he never regained his skills sufficiently to play at the major league level again. A teammate of Crespi's was outfielder Enos "Country" Slaughter, famous for his all-out hustle on the base paths and in the field. George "Whitey" Kurowski emerged as a starter at third base for the Cardinals in 1942 at the age of 24 and remained there until the end of the decade. Of course, the cornerstone of the Cardinals dynasty in the 1940s was player whose nickname was simply, "The Man," but there was nothing simple about Stan Musial's abilities as a ballplayer.

Nicknames seem to have lost some creativity in recent decades. The great Bob Gibson was sometimes referred to as "Gibby" or "Hoot," Orlando Cepeda was labeled "Cha-Cha" and "Baby Bull," and Lou Brock was "The Franchise," but otherwise nicknames were in short supply. The flashy teams of the 1980s did a little better with Ozzie "Wizard of Oz" Smith, Lonnie "Skates" Smith, and Vince "Vincent Van Go" Coleman. The latest Cardinals superstar, Albert Pujols, is so proficient with the bat that he has had several nicknames attached to him, including "Prince Albert" and "Phat Albert." "The Man" was already taken, so this Latino slugger had to settle for the Spanish equivalent, "El Hombre."

Like many of their players, Cardinals managers have also had their share of colorful names—both literally and figuratively. Albert "Red" Schoendienst and Dorrel "Whitey" Herzog led the Redbirds to championships in the 1960s and 1980s respectively, and they were preceded by other skippers such as Charles "Gabby" Street, Solomon "Solly" Hemus, and going back to the turn of the century, Charles "Kid" Nichols.

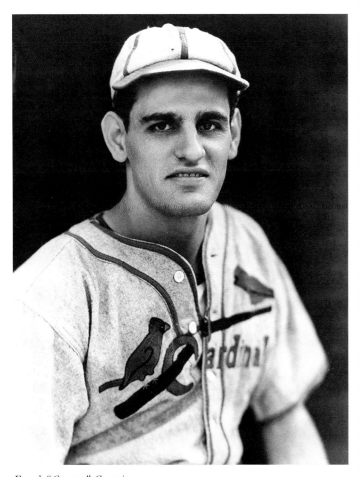

Frank "Creepy" Crespi

Orlando "Cha-Cha" Cepeda, October 1968

Above: *Bob "Hoot" Gibson, Stan "The Man" Musial, Albert "Red" Schoendienst, and Lou "The Franchise" Brock, at Busch Stadium, 1996*

Left: *Charles "Kid" Nichols, 1905*

Joe Garagiola, 1951

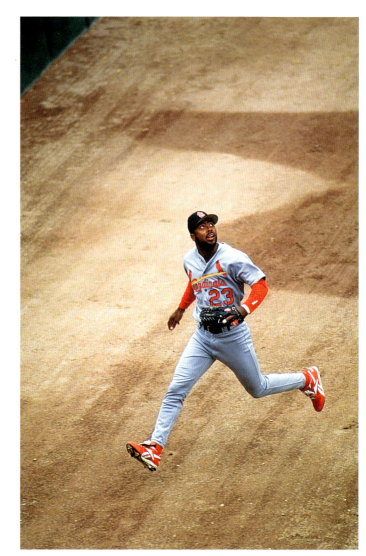

Bernard Gilkey, 1995

Homegrown Heroes

The Cardinals roster over the years has featured numerous St. Louis native sons, and many other local products have gone on to star for other major league teams.

Along with some of the world's best Italian dishes, the Hill neighborhood in St. Louis has also produced (at the very least) two quality catchers for the game of baseball. The two men were born nine months apart in the mid-1920s, and one of them stayed near home to play for the Cardinals. Lawrence "Yogi" Berra would claim three American League Most Valuable Player Awards and ten World Series championship rings during his Hall of Fame career with the New York Yankees. (Incidentally, the man who would succeed Berra as the Yankees' catcher—Elston Howard—also was from St. Louis.) While not compiling the impressive career statistics that Berra did, fellow Hill native Joe Garagiola nonetheless proved himself as a clutch player. He was a main contributor in the World Series win over the Red Sox in 1946 with his .316 average and 4 RBI during the seven games. Other contemporaries of Garagiola, such as Frank "Creepy" Crespi and Dick Sisler, were St. Louis natives as well. A few years later, St. Louis native Charlie James was part of the run to the 1964 championship, as was Mike Shannon of south St. Louis.

St. Louisan Bernard Gilkey, who graduated from the same University City High School as former Cardinals General Manager

Vaughan "Bing" Devine, was part of a budding outfield triumvirate at Busch Stadium, along with Brian Jordan and Ray Lankford, in the mid-1990s before being dealt to the New York Mets in early 1996. Great things were also expected of third baseman Scott Cooper, a St. Louis and Pattonville High School product who was acquired from the Red Sox in 1995. Cooper had been an all-star the previous two seasons in Boston but wasn't able to produce for his hometown team, batting .230 during his one year in a Cardinals uniform. He played 75 games for Kansas City in his final major league season in 1997 after spending a year playing in Japan.

In addition to his baseball talents, outfielder Kerry Robinson developed quite a reputation as an amateur hockey player while growing up on the north side of St. Louis. A graduate of Hazelwood East High School, Robinson was selected by the Cardinals in the 1995 draft after playing at Southeast Missouri State University. He spent the majority of the next five seasons in the minor league systems of the Tampa Bay Devil Rays, Seattle Mariners, Cincinnati Reds, and New York Yankees. By 2000, he was back in the Cardinals organization, however, and a year later he landed a roster spot with the parent club.

Native St. Louisan and Vianney High School graduate Cliff Politte pitched for the Cardinals in 1998 (and threw the very first pitch at the Cardinals' new spring training home, Roger Dean Stadium in Jupiter, Florida) and would later hurl for the 2005 World Series champion Chicago White Sox. In 2008, another St. Louis native, Kyle McClellan—a graduate of Hazelwood West High School—appeared in 68 games as a key member of the Cardinals relief corps.

Kyle McClellan, 2008

The Gas House Gang enjoying a lighter moment

Bad Boys

At various points throughout their history, the Cardinals have shown themselves to be a microcosm of the American Midwest, representative of the fighting spirit of the common man. As such, the Gas House Gang Cardinals of the 1930s became one of Depression-era America's greatest collection of heroes, a group of underpaid men who scratched, clawed, and fought their way to the top against long odds. Known for their dirty and torn uniforms, tobacco juice dribbling from their mouths, and their seemingly nonstop taunting of the opposing teams and umpires, the Gas House Gang precipitated a reign of spikes-high terror on the rest of the National League, racing to the pennant in 1934 and a seven-game triumph over the Detroit Tigers in the World Series. Interestingly, they actually received their nickname the following year, when New York writer Dan Daniel used his cartoon to liken the Cardinals' appearance to boys from the "Gas House" district of town. Daniel wished that his boys, who lived on the "nice" side of the tracks—presumably the New York Giants—would be a bit more like the rough-and-tumble Cardinals of that day, one of the most competitive teams ever assembled.

A leading member of the Gas House Gang was Joe Medwick, well-known as one of the toughest guys on a team full of tough individuals. While ultimately remembered for his hitting, Medwick was originally known for his two nicknames, "Muscles" and "Ducky." He obviously preferred the former, which described his strong body, and hated the latter, which had been laid upon him at a minor league game by a female fan who likened his running style to that of a feathered friend. Whether from this or other sources, Medwick was quite defensive and never met a pitch or a fight he did not like—a free swinger in both regards. Medwick came to Dizzy Dean's defense when he was verbally assaulted by columnist Mike Miley and his friend, former pro football player and writer Irv Kupcinet, in a Tampa hotel in the mid-1930s. With insults flying back and forth, Medwick let fly with a right cross that caught "Kup" on the chin and sent him sprawling back into a large potted plant in the hotel lobby, causing a domino-like destruction of other plants in the room. This was a rare occurrence, however, in which Medwick was not fighting Dizzy himself—scraps that often took place right in the dugout.

Joe Medwick sliding hard into catcher Mickey Cochrane, 1934 World Series

James "Tex" Carleton (second from left) and Dizzy Dean (second from right) as teammates, 1932

Joaquin Andujar being restrained by teammates during Game Seven, 1985 World Series

Like his teammate Medwick, James "Tex" Carleton did not enjoy being second fiddle to Dizzy on the roster, and by 1934, it was clear that he was sitting behind both Dizzy and Paul Dean in the pitching rotation. When Carleton was traded to the pennant-winning Cubs in 1935, the animosity between him and Dizzy boiled over in a game at Sportsman's Park in late summer. Carleton, not pitching that day, was berating Dean from the dugout all afternoon long, and by the fifth inning, Dizzy had heard enough. He stomped from the pitching mound halfway toward the Cubs' dugout and challenged Carleton to a fight. Carleton charged him, but each was restrained before the two could come to blows.

George Hendrick, a power-hitting outfielder from the 1970s and early 1980s, has often been credited with starting the modern trend of wearing baseball pants stretched down to the ankles. In another example of being ahead of his time, Hendrick was also among the pioneers of a modern baseball ritual, followed by many players, of saying little or nothing to the sportswriters and other media. Often characterizing himself as misunderstood, Hendrick's mute approach led broadcaster Jack Buck to dub him "Silent George." "He didn't talk to the media," Buck recalled in his book *That's a Winner!* "That didn't bother me. In fact, I had fun with it. I tried three or four times to make a polite approach and ask him to do an interview, but he wouldn't do it. So I started calling him Silent George. The listeners knew what it was all about. I think even Hendrick enjoyed the nickname."

Pitcher Joaquin Andujar was known for inciting incidents during his excursions to the pitching mound. At a game in St. Louis on June 18, 1983, Bill Buckner of the Chicago Cubs homered off Andujar in the first inning. Upon rounding third, Buckner looked at Andujar and gave him a pistol point with his finger and thumb, a response to the cocky pitcher in mimicking what Andujar often had done after striking out a batter. The result was another bench-clearing melee between the Cards and Cubs.

Andujar's temper and competitive fire was one detraction from the great Cardinals teams of the 1980s; yet another was the seedy reputation of a couple of the club's outfielders from the same time period. Entangled in the ugly drug inquiry of this era was Lonnie Smith, whose departure to the Kansas City Royals in 1985 would make room for Vince Coleman in the St. Louis outfield. While his batting ability and running speed were never questioned, Smith seemed destined for American League play given his defensive inconsistencies. Smith, however, was beloved by Whitey Herzog, and Herzog wished he'd had a place for him. "I'll say this," Whitey asserted after the trade was made. "If we had the designated hitter in the National League, Lonnie would've died a Cardinal."

David Green, 1982 World Series

The Cardinals management had originally envisioned that Smith would be a long-term partner with another talented young player in the Busch Stadium outfield, David Green. After enjoying a fine first full season in the majors during the Cards' 1982 championship run, Green was soon battling problems with alcohol. Perpetually at odds with authority figures, Green was dealt to the San Francisco Giants before the 1985 season. After the trade, Herzog summed up the frustrations surrounding Green's failed potential. "If David would wake up one morning and say, 'I'm going to do it,' there's no telling what he could do."

Hard-Luck Players

Bill Delancey took the National League by storm as a rookie catcher in 1934, splitting time with veteran Virgil Davis behind the plate for St. Louis' Gas House Gang. A big, strong young man with left-handed-hitting power, Delancey batted .316 with 13 homers in 93 games for the Cardinals and was envisioned as a fixture at the position in St. Louis for years to come. Branch Rickey believed that Delancey was one of the top catching prospects of all time. By the end of the 1935 season, however, the young backstop was complaining of excessive fatigue, and doctors discovered that he had contracted tuberculosis. He was out of baseball for the next four years before attempting a comeback in 1940, but he would play in only 15 games, never to return to the majors. Delancey passed away from the disease on his birthday, November 28, 1946, at the age of 35.

Although fellow catcher Darrell Porter had a long and successful career in the major leagues, ultimately his story had a sad and premature ending. After coming across the state from the Kansas City Royals in 1981, the Missouri native quickly established himself as a clutch player for the Cardinals. A four-time all-star before arriving in St. Louis, Porter would take home the World Series Most Valuable Player trophy during the Cards' 1982 triumph over the Milwaukee Brewers, the team with which Porter had broken into the majors as a 19-year-old in 1971. Drug and alcohol problems haunted the talented player through much of his career, but Porter appeared to have conquered his substance abuse by the time he entered his new life after baseball, spending time speaking to youth groups and church organizations. Unfortunately, Porter was found dead near his car on August 5, 2002 in the Kansas City suburb of Sugar Creek, Missouri, with an autopsy revealing he died from the "toxic effects of cocaine." He was 50 years old.

On June 22 of that same year, the Cardinals and the Cubs were scheduled to play each other at Wrigley Field at 1:20 p.m. When the stadium clock showed 1:35 and no Cardinals players were present in the visiting dugout, a murmur began to drift throughout the ballpark. Manager Tony La Russa soon emerged from the tunnel, wearing his uniform pants, socks, and shoes but only a t-shirt and no jersey, obviously unprepared for a ballgame. He walked slowly toward the umpires at home plate with his head down and his hands tucked in his back pockets, said something briefly to the umpires, and solemnly returned to the locker room. Cardinals pitcher Darryl Kile, who was scheduled to start the next day's game and thus had been granted permission to arrive at the ballpark separately from his teammates, had been late in arriving to Wrigley. Phone calls to his hotel room went unanswered, and when authorities checked his room they found that Kile had passed away. Word of what had occurred soon spread through the ballpark grandstand, and the game was postponed for another date. The two teams voted to play the following game on Sunday night, the 23rd. The autopsy later revealed that Kile, age 33, had died from coronary atherosclerosis, or a narrowing of the arteries supplying the heart muscle.

Darrell Porter celebrating after the 1982 World Series

Darryl Kile acknowledging the crowd, April 2001

Members of the Cardinals during a moment of silence honoring Darryl Kile, June 25, 2002

Josh Hancock's jersey hanging in the Cardinals bullpen, April 30, 2007

Rick Ankiel pitching, April 2000

Pitcher Josh Hancock was picked up by the Cardinals early in the 2006 season after bouncing around with several organizations, most recently being cast off by the Cincinnati Reds before that year's spring training. Looking for depth in their bullpen, the Cards were willing to give Hancock a chance. He responded by pitching in 62 games for St. Louis during the regular season and three more in the playoffs, before sitting on the bench for the entire 2006 World Series win by the Cardinals over Detroit. Hancock and followers of the team looked forward to an increased role for the young righty on the staff the following year.

On the Saturday afternoon of April 28, 2007, at Busch Stadium, Hancock threw three innings of mop-up duty in an 8–1 pummeling of the Cardinals by the Cubs. That evening, the inconspicuous troubles with which Hancock had been battling finally came to fatal fruition. Driving westbound on Highway 40 through St. Louis, Hancock's sport utility vehicle veered onto the left shoulder and struck a stationary flatbed tow truck that was in the process of assisting a disabled vehicle. Hancock died instantly. Police reports showed that his blood-alcohol content was 0.157, nearly twice the legal driving limit in Missouri. In addition, police stated that Hancock had been trying to send a text message over his cellular phone at the time of the crash, had not been wearing a seat belt, and was traveling 68 miles per hour in a 55-mph zone. According to the *St. Louis Post-Dispatch*, three days earlier Hancock's teammates had become concerned when he failed to respond to repeated phone messages left for him when he was late to a Cardinals game. As with Kile, DeLancey, and other losses from the Cardinals family over the years, a pall of sadness shrouded the team.

A hard-luck story that has a happy ending is that of Rick Ankiel, one of the most amazing stories of transformation in the history of baseball. After being selected by the Cardinals in the second round of the 1997 amateur draft as a Florida prep phenom, Ankiel arrived in the team's minor league system and was quickly hailed as the top left-handed pitching prospect in the game. In 1999, the 19-year-old was the youngest player in the big leagues. In 2000, he broke Dean's club record for strikeouts by a rookie pitcher, with 194. Ankiel's professional pitching world suddenly unraveled in that season's playoffs, however. Unable to find the plate, he walked 11 batters in just four innings, with several pitches missing the catcher altogether. After permitting 25 walks in 24 innings in 2001, Ankiel was out of Major League Baseball, returning briefly in 2004 to pitch 10 more innings.

Rick Ankiel, April 2001

Rick Ankiel making a diving catch in the outfield, 2008

The Cardinals coaching staff always knew that Ankiel could hit well, since he had been a dominant offensive player in the Florida amateur leagues in addition to being a top-shelf pitcher. Virtually out of options to return to pitching, Ankiel and the Cardinals turned their attention to transforming him into an outfielder. He succeeded, and by 2007—ten years after he first joined the organization—Ankiel was a starting outfielder for the St. Louis Cardinals, hitting long balls as if he was born to do so and gracefully gliding along the center field grass to snare fly balls. He belted 13 home runs in just 172 at bats in 2007 and added 25 more in a full campaign in 2008.

Superstitions and Musical Beats

During the Great Depression in the 1930s, even major league ballplayers had to be economical with their entertainment expenses, and in many respects, Pepper Martin was representative of how life was during these difficult times. Before his years of stardom with the Cardinals, Martin would hop from town to town on trains essentially as a hobo, looking for a place to play ball. (Later, he would afford himself the luxury of a used pickup truck, and he was often seen driving with his two hunting dogs bouncing around with him in the front seat.) During the baseball offseasons, he would hunt rattlesnakes with his wife for the St. Louis Zoo, arming themselves with only a forked stick and a canvas bag. And when the Cardinals went on the road, he would fire up the makeshift Musical Mudcat Band composed of himself and several of his teammates. "I was perhaps the only manager who carried an orchestra," Frankie Frisch said of his days in charge of the loony bunch. "We traveled with more instruments than we did shirts or anything else."

With Martin humming away on his harmonica, Lon Warneke, Stan "Frenchy" Bordagaray, Bill McGee, and Bob Weiland (as well as other substitutes over the years) chimed in with their own homemade hardware, be it tapping the spoons, scratching the washboard, or blowing the jug.

Slightly more refined was the harmonica talent that Stan Musial brought to the clubhouse in the 1940s. This era also began

Pepper Martin (front) and his Musical Mudcat Band (left to right): Lon Warneke, Dick Siebert, Ray Harrell, Herb Bremer, Jimmy Brown, and Bill McGee

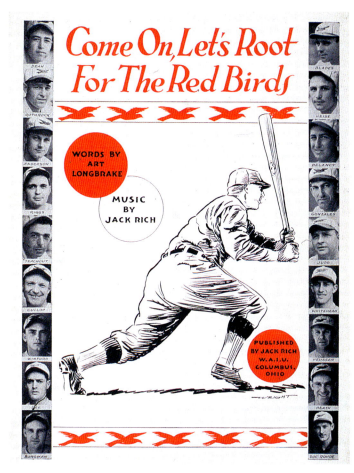

Gas House Gang St. Louis Cardinals Sheet Music, 1935

the tradition of superstitious songs, tunes played in the Cardinals clubhouse every day when the team was on a winning streak. Among the favorites Musial remembered was the old Spike Jones melody "Pass the Biscuits Mirandy," which he was happy to whip out on a moment's notice. In later years, Lou Brock would spin "Fistful of Dollars" on the record player in the locker room after a victory, with first baseman Orlando Cepeda dancing on top of the trunk where players locked up their valuables during the game. Cepeda and Brock's Cardinals of those days carried on many other superstitions as well, such as the "Tomato-Rice Soup Ball." One of the players' wives had made tomato and rice soup before a game, which led to a winning streak. When the streak was over, Cepeda decided to paint an old baseball half-red and use it in the soup's place as the team's new object of reverence, insisting that this same ball be used for infield practice before every inning of every game (and to be caught only by assistant coach Dick Sisler when thrown into the dugout by Cepeda) until the next winning stretch was halted.

Since 1971, music within the confines of Busch Stadium has been led by the unmistakable sounds of Ernie Hays on the electric organ, which greets folks with such beloved tunes such as "Meet Me in St. Louie" or the Budweiser theme, "Here Comes the King." Hays continued to provide the background notes after the team moved into the new Busch Stadium in downtown St. Louis.

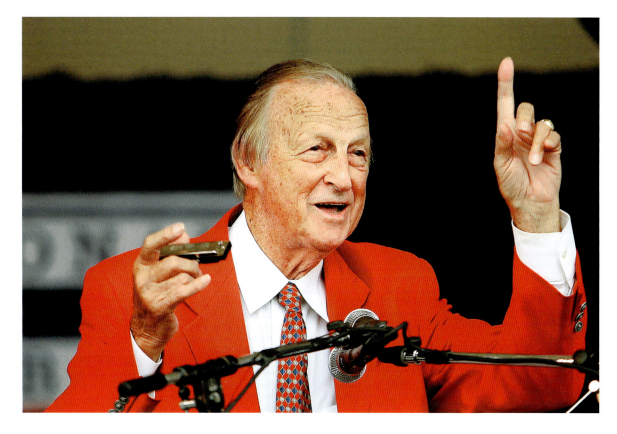

Stan Musial entertaining the crowd at the Baseball Hall of Fame, 2005

Uniforms and Equipment

One day when the St. Louis baseball team took the field about a century ago, a woman in the stands noted the bright red color on its uniforms. A local writer took note of the comment, and from his article the St. Louis entry soon became known as the "Cardinals." Cardinal red has certainly been a staple of the team uniform ever since.

Through the years, many changes have passed through the Cardinals and the city. However, another constant has been the "birds on the bat," the trademark logo of the Cardinals that dates back to the early 1900s. It has long been a source of pride for the players. "When I put on that jersey, with those birds on the bat," shortstop Marty Marion once asserted, "I felt like I had the winning way."

Other than a few years during the 1910s and 1920s when red pinstripes were added, Cardinals uniforms remained fairly consistent through the 75 years of the twentieth century: white home uniforms and gray road uniforms. In 1927, the club donned special jerseys with the words "World Champions" emblazoned on the left breast and only the "St. L" abbreviation on the sleeve to provide a clue as to which team it was. By the late 1930s, the Cardinals added a zipper front to their jerseys, deviating temporarily from the traditional pullover or button-down style. This would be coupled with the incorporation of

Elton "Icebox" Chamberlain, St. Louis Browns, 1889

Roger Bresnahan, 1911

Grover Cleveland Alexander with two flappers, 1927

Below: *Pepper Martin, circa 1930*

more blue into the uniform in the 1940s, namely in the long-sleeve undershirts and the caps. In the 1950s, a simpler uniform made a brief appearance without the birds-on-the-bat logo, an idea that was quickly discarded. Uniform numbers were added to the front of the jersey in the early 1960s. The buttonless pullover jersey was introduced in 1971, but a return to traditional, retro-styles uniforms in the 1990s brought back the button-down front.

In 1976, the Cardinals joined other National League teams in celebrating the 100-year anniversary of the circuit with original-style caps, which offered tribute to the league's founding fathers with striped hats. In a symbol of the zany 1970s, the Cardinals (as well as the Chicago Cubs and a handful of other teams) opted for powder-blue road uniforms. They returned to the traditional gray-based travel jersey and pants in 1985.

Like Penn State University in football or UCLA in basketball, Cardinals uniforms have long been majestic in their simplicity and generally unwavering style, setting a standard of class in the at-times-turbulent arena of sport-uniform fashion.

Ken Boyer, circa 1963

Lou Brock, 1976

Harry Walker, 1944

Albert Pujols, circa 2005

St. Louis Browns at the first Sportsman's Park, 1884

The Ballparks

Aerial view of Sportsman's Park, 1926

The first ballpark that served as the home field for the St. Louis Brown Stockings of the American Association was known as Sportsman's Park, although it was a different structure than the one in which the Cardinals played for nearly half a century. The original Sportsman's, which also went by the name of Grand Avenue Ball Grounds, had been used by amateur and early professional baseball teams as far back as the late 1860s. When the Browns were formed in 1882, they moved in to the wooden ballpark at the intersection of Grand and Dodier.

The Browns were one of four American Association teams absorbed by the National League in 1892, and the following season the club began playing at a new ballpark located a few blocks away, at the corner of Natural Bridge and Vandeventer Avenues. Originally called New Sportsman's Park, it was later renamed Robison Field in honor of the club's owner at the time,

Stanley Robison. Perhaps the most distinctive feature of Robison Field was the "shoot the chutes" amusement park ride that sat for a time beyond the right-center field wall.

The Cardinals played at Robison Field until 1920, when financially strapped owner Sam Breadon sold the ballpark. The team relocated to the new Sportsman's Park, which had been built by the American League Browns in 1902 on virtually the same site as the original ballpark of that name. (The Robison Field site was later taken over by Beaumont High School.)

For many years, students at St. Louis University would make the trek north up Grand Boulevard—by street car or by foot—to the corner of Grand Avenue and Dodier Street, where from April to September a Major League Baseball game was being played nearly every day. With a team in both major leagues until 1954, the city always had baseball on its mind. Sportsman's Park accommodated about 18,000 fans at the time the Cardinals moved in, and as the fortunes of both teams began to rise (the Browns finished one game out of first place in 1922 while the Cardinals were in the midst of a heated pennant race for much of that same season), the ballpark's capacity was nearly doubled, to 34,000, with a major renovation in 1925.

Postcard view of Sportsman's Park, 1954

One of the more interesting features of Sportsman's Park was the title of ownership. The Browns—traditionally the weaker team on the field—were the landlords while the Cardinals were the tenants.

Aerial view of Busch Stadium II, circa 1966

Aerial view of Busch Stadium II with new Busch Stadium III under construction, 2004

After Gussie Busch purchased the Cardinals in 1953, Browns owner Bill Veeck, knowing that his own team was on its way out, sold the ballpark to Busch. The new Cards owner wanted to rename it Budweiser Park, but league officials opined that a name involving an alcoholic beverage might be uncouth, and Busch was forced to settle for his own surname. The structure was rechristened Busch Stadium—which, of course, still promoted one of Anheuser-Busch's other beer brands, Busch.

Among the ballpark's special physical attributes was the simple flag pole, which oddly stood in play in front of the center field wall (until about 1950). Additionally, when the short distance to the right field wall started resulting in too many cheap home runs, a 25-foot-high wire screen was placed atop the brick wall in front of the right field bleachers. (When Jimmie Foxx of the Philadelphia A's belted 58 home runs in 1932, it was estimated that he knocked another 12 balls against the screen at Sportsman's Park—thus he would have notched 70 home runs for the season had St. Louis maintained its pre-1929 confines.)

Plans for a comprehensive reconstruction of downtown St. Louis had been in the works for decades but did not come to fruition until the mid-1960s under Mayor Alfonso Cervantes. Rising simultaneously on the banks of the Mississippi River were the 630-foot Gateway Arch (to commemorate the westward expansion of the United States) and the Civic Center Memorial Stadium, as the new sports facility was awkwardly known. Quickly renamed Busch Stadium—referred to by some as Busch Stadium II to distinguish it from Sportsman's Park's era with that name—the ballpark was designed to be one of the new multipurpose arenas that were being built around the country to house multiple professional sports. (The stadium would be home to the St. Louis Cardinals of the National Football League as well, just as Sportsman's Park had been after the football team migrated from Chicago in 1960.) The most recognizable feature of the new Busch Stadium was the interlocking of 96 miniature arches that encircled the top of the stadium, which clearly set Busch apart from its architectural brothers in Philadelphia, Cincinnati, and Pittsburgh and gave it a uniquely St. Louisan flair.

Aerial view of Busch Stadium III, 2006

Busch Stadium II, 2005

Busch Stadium III, 2006

Final game at Busch Stadium II, October 19, 2005

With the construction of a domed stadium to house the newly arriving Rams football team in the mid-1990s (the football Cardinals has departed for Phoenix in 1988), Busch Stadium underwent a major overhaul to transform it into a baseball-only facility. The seating capacity was reduced from nearly 60,000 to 49,676 with the removal of the distant upper-deck seats in center field, and a new scoreboard and championship display were constructed in their place. Additionally, the bullpens were removed from the foul-line area and placed behind the outfield wall.

Although the 1996 renovation introduced many improvements and updates to the 30-year-old stadium, plans were soon in the works for a new, retro-styled ballpark for the Cardinals. On a site immediately adjacent to the existing stadium, ground was broken for the new facility in January 2004, and work proceeded over the next two years. The Cardinals played their final game at the old Busch Stadium on October 19, 2005, against the Houston Astros in Game Six of the National League Championship Series.

The latest Busch Stadium (called in some circles "Busch Stadium III") opened for business in April 2006. Featuring both classical ballpark elements and the most modern conveniences, Busch was an instant hit with the fans, with every game that first season a sellout. In contrast to the fully enclosed configuration of its predecessor, the open outfield at Busch Stadium III offers glorious views of the downtown skyline and the Gateway Arch. With fewer than 47,000 seats, the new facility offers a more intimate environment than the old multipurpose stadium, and its sightlines and construction are geared to maximize the baseball-watching experience. It also honors past Cardinals heroes, with statues of Stan Musial, Enos Slaughter, Red Schoendienst, Bob Gibson, Lou Brock, Ozzie Smith, and others near the entrances of the ballpark.

Cardinals lining up for the national anthem at the first game at Busch Stadium III, April 10, 2006

Entrance to Busch Stadium III

The Playing Field and Outfield Dimensions

As with most early ballparks, St. Louis' Robison Field was built to fit within the confines of the urban streets that surrounded it. As such, its outfield dimensions were extremely asymmetrical in the park's original configuration: 470 feet to left field, 500 feet to straightaway center, and a mere 290 to right field. In the days of the dead ball, the spacious left-center field area provided ample opportunity for extra-base hits and inside-the-park homers, except when overflow crowds were accommodated in a roped-off area on the outfield itself. The construction of new grandstands in 1909 reined in Robison's dimensions a bit. The distance to left field was reduced to 380 feet, and the center field wall was then 435 feet from home plate.

Like Robison, Sportsman's Park's playing field was also deepest in left-center, while the wall angled in sharply to make for a short right field, measuring in at just under 310 feet in the ballpark's final configuration. The Busch Stadium that opened in 1966 reflected the symmetrical layout common among the multipurpose facilities of that era. At 330 feet down the lines and 414 feet to dead center, however, the dimensions were ideal for the fleet-footed, strong-pitching Cardinals teams of the 1960s and 1980s.

The condition of the playing surface at Sportsman's Park was a source of regular frustration on the part of players from both the American and National Leagues. The main reason behind the sub-par condition of the field was that, because Sportsman's served as the home to teams from both circuits, it was in use on an almost-daily basis during the season, and thus the grounds crew had little opportunity to work on maintaining the grass and infield dirt.

When the Cardinals moved into new Busch Stadium in 1966, they were greeted with a well-manicured natural grass field, which at the time was the surface utilized everywhere except in the strange indoor ecosystem of the Astrodome in Houston. By the end of the decade, more teams were exploring the idea of artificial playing surfaces even for outdoor facilities, and Busch Stadium joined the surge, installing the synthetic grass in 1970. After research displayed a greater tendency for injuries on artificial playing surfaces (and after the St. Louis Rams moved out of Busch Stadium and into their own domed stadium for football), the Cardinals opted to switch back to natural grass in 1996 during the conversion of Busch Stadium to a baseball-only facility.

Although it had little to do with the greater wear-and-tear on the body brought about by artificial turf, the synthetic surface at old Busch Stadium did indirectly lead to one famous casualty. Prior to the fourth game of the 1985 National League Championship Series against the Dodgers, fleet outfielder Vince Coleman got his leg caught in the machine that automatically rolled up the rain tarpaulin. The rookie Coleman—who had dazzled with 110 stolen bases during the regular season—was forced to miss the remainder of the playoffs with a bone chip and heavy bruises.

While the latest Busch Stadium that opened in 2006 reintroduced many of the qualities of the classic ballparks, such as a natural grass playing surface, the outfield maintained the symmetrical dimensions utilized at the multipurpose Busch. Although it is slightly deeper down the foul lines (335 feet), the power alleys and center field are comparable to what was found in its predecessor.

Aerial view of playing surface and dimensions, Sportsman's Park

Natural grass playing surface at Busch Stadium II, circa 1967

Artificial turf playing surface at Busch Stadium II, 1995

Playing surface and dimensions at Busch Stadium III

The Dugouts, Clubhouses, and Bullpens

Just as visiting and Cardinals players alike often complained about the condition of the playing field at Sportsman's Park, the dugout and clubhouse facilities also left much to be desired. Cramped and lacking many basic amenities, the locker rooms were a far cry from the high-tech digs that are found in many ballparks today. Perhaps no one was more aware of this than Jerry Gibson, the Cardinals' longtime batboy. Gibson cleaned the locker rooms and umpire quarters at Sportsman's and was with the club in the mid-1960s when it made its transition from the stadium on Grand Avenue and Dodier Street to the more modern Busch Stadium downtown. The facilities for players and umpires were further upgraded with the construction of the third Busch Stadium in 2006.

The earliest facilities that housed baseball matches in the late-nineteenth and early-twentieth centuries usually lacked dedicated spaces for the players to wait between innings or for a pitcher to warm up. Dugouts were generally simple wooden benches on the sidelines, and the bullpen was any place the pitcher could find to practice his fastball away from innocent bystanders. Gradually, permanent dugouts were introduced to ballparks, and dedicated bullpen areas were set up near the corners of the foul territory in left and right field. When Busch Stadium was converted from multipurpose to baseball-only use in 1996, the bullpens were moved behind the outfield walls. The current Busch Stadium also tucks the bullpens behind the outfield walls in left-center and right-center.

Cardinals players relaxing in the locker room at their spring training facility in St. Petersburg, Florida

Darrell Porter relaxing in the Busch Stadium locker room, 1981

Jackie Robinson (#42) passing through the Cardinals dugout to get to the clubhouse, September 1949

Cardinals players in the dugout at Busch Stadium II, 1987

Cardinals players in the dugout at Busch Stadium III, 2006

The Scoreboards and Billboards

Colorful scoreboards, scorecards, and their adjoining advertisements have long been a part of the game-day experience in St. Louis. The many signs covering the outfield wall at Sportsman's Park hawked everything from booze and cigarettes (Falstaff and Alpen Brau beers, Old Quaker Whiskey, and Chesterfield cigarettes, to name just a few) to household products and clothing (Sayman's and Life Buoy soaps, Gem razor blades, Winthrop Shoes, and much more). When signs on the outfield wall went out of vogue for a time, the ads were placed high above the playing surface. Adorning the advertising upper-tier sections near the Busch Stadium scoreboard were ads for Schnucks supermarkets, Steak 'n' Shake and The Pasta House restaurants, and of course the obligatory nonstop mentions of Anheuser-Busch products.

With most modern major league teams doing whatever they can to squeeze out an extra nickel, advertisements on the walls encircling the playing field have made a comeback in recent years. As with many of the newer parks around the National and American Leagues, the new Busch Stadium has fallen into the culture of text messages on the scoreboard to loved ones, video games for kids, and nearly any other activity imaginable—all available in addition to watching the game itself.

Scoreboards and billboards at Busch Stadium II, 2005

Scoreboard and billboards at Sportsman's Park, circa 1952

Scoreboards and billboards at Busch Stadium III

The Fans

"Nothing bleeds quite like devotion," as Gary Kissick once wrote, and the lifeblood of Cardinals fans runs wide and deep. Its foundation is well-anchored, in part, due simply to the historical nature of the major leagues. Until the westward movement of the Giants and Dodgers to California in the late 1950s and the expansion of both leagues soon to follow in the 1960s (with the National League adding Houston and Atlanta), St. Louis had been the southern-most and western-most city in the major leagues. As a result, the Cardinals developed a fan base that stretched from the Gateway City to the Gulf of Mexico and all points in between. As the character in John Grisham's novel *A Painted House* attests, a family sitting on their front porch in Arkansas, listening to the Cardinals on the radio, felt as close to the action as those lucky fans sitting in Sportsman's Park.

Left: *Overflow crowd watching from the sidelines of the field at Sportsman's Park, mid-1930s*

Fans cheering at Sportsman's Park during the 1946 World Series

The Cardinals' fan base remains amazingly strong today, in spite of the relatively small major league market that encompasses the St. Louis area and the lack of a coast-to-coast superstation on cable to cover the team, such as the Chicago Cubs enjoy and the Atlanta Braves utilized for years. No team's collection of fans is more loyal to wearing the home-team colors on game day than those of the Cards, as Busch Stadium is regularly filled with red-clad fans enjoying traditions such as the Clydesdale horses trotting onto the field with Budweiser wagon and boxes in tow.

In the 1950s and before, a trip to a Cardinals game meant a streetcar ride up Grand Boulevard, or perhaps a stroll alongside those very streetcars to the ballpark. Like contemporaries Wrigley Field in Chicago or Crosley Field in Cincinnati, Sportsman's Park was a neighborhood stadium, formerly alive with thriving businesses, bustling sidewalks, and a general hum of activity. The stadium was the focal point of neighborhood life, and it sprung up seemingly out of nowhere for the excited fan visiting for the first time.

Fans storming the field after the Cardinals won in the 1982 World Series

Fans celebrating a Cardinal win in the 2006 World Series

Fans file in to Busch Stadium II, Opening Day 2004

As the team moved from its north-city location to downtown, a modern game-night in St. Louis has become a different, yet as unmistakable, picture: numerous cars (and later, cars joined by Metrolink trains) converging toward the downtown area at the river, funneling in from West County and Illinois (also known as the Metro East), and all points in between and beyond. While Cardinal red is of course the color of choice around the city, it darkens with thickness around the riverfront when the Cardinals are on the home schedule. Fans are greeted nearly everywhere by Budweiser signs and reminders of the glory decades and teams past, with numerous championship pennants waving high in the breeze.

Whether at Sportsman's Park or one of the Busch Stadiums, the atmosphere felt within the confines of a St. Louis ballpark is different than that felt in other cities' ballparks, exuding great focus and elation. Cardinals fans have a scholarly appreciation for the game that is mixed with an unbridled enthusiasm. There are no better fans in baseball, and Cardinals followers know it.

When the game lets out at the end of the evening, most of the fans disperse out of the ballpark east or west to one of the two parking garages that adjoin the stadium; others filter out north, toward the after-game conversation at Mike Shannon's restaurant, the downtown hotels, or perhaps a late-night cold one on Laclede's Landing. Still others exit to the south, walking down Seventh Street toward the blues and jazz sounds of the historic Soulard neighborhood. When the fans leave, the downtown area stunningly returns to a quiet, almost small-town feel.

Fans outside the gates of Busch Stadium III, Opening Day 2006

The Budweiser Clydesdales circle the field at Busch Stadium III, Opening Day 2006

Fredbird, the Cardinals' mascot, leading the cheers at Busch Stadium III, 2006

National League All-Star Team, 1933

THE CARDINALS AND THE ALL-STAR GAME

With its galaxy of top players over the years, the Cardinals have held a standing post in the annual Midsummer Classic, the Major League Baseball All-Star Game. Since the event's inception in 1933, St. Louis has played host in 1940, 1948, 1957, and 1966, and will again in 2009. (The Cardinals were designated as the host team in 1940, while the Browns took the role in 1948.) The 1966 designation of the All-Star Game to St. Louis was in recognition of the opening of a new ballpark. Only three months old in July 1966, the stars were greeted with vintage St. Louis summer heat on the day of the game, with temperatures reaching 115 degrees on the field. When asked of his thoughts of the new stadium, honorary manager Casey Stengel was heard to mutter, "It sure holds the heat well."

Several Cardinals players have had notable moments in All-Star Game play. Pepper Martin and Frankie Frisch took the first two at-bats in All-Star Game history at Chicago's Comiskey Park in 1933, while Cardinals hurler Bill Hallahan became the National League's first-ever starting pitcher in the bottom half of that first inning. Four years later, Dizzy Dean endured a career-changing incident at the All-Star Game in Washington, as a line drive off the bat of Cleveland's Earl Averill struck Dean on the big toe of the left foot, breaking the bone. Dean (who had also started the 1935 All-Star Game for the National League against Lefty Gomez of the Yankees) was always anxious to take the mound, and he returned to action sooner than physicians suggested. Not able to place his full weight on the foot, Dean altered his pitching motion to a point that irreversibly hurt his arm, leading to his early retirement in 1941 at the age of 31.

The National League squad for the 1966 contest featured just three players from the hometown team, although Bob Gibson was named to the team but did not play. The game was won by the

Senior Circuit in 10 innings, with St. Louis' own Tim McCarver sliding in with the winning run.

Stan Musial posted a .317 career mark with 6 home runs in his 24 All-Star Game appearances, while his close friend Red Schoendienst won the 1950 contest for the National League with a fourteenth-inning homer off Ted Gray of the Detroit Tigers. However, since the award was first presented in 1962, no member of the Cardinals has been named All-Star Game Most Valuable Player.

Right: *Field-level view, 1966 All-Star Game*

Below: *Tim McCarver scoring the winning run, 1966 All-Star Game*

Voices of the Cardinals

For many years, igniting the souls of St. Louisans and fans throughout the Midwest were the voices heard on the mighty 50,000-watt "Voice of St. Louis," KMOX. In the new century, other stations have taken over the radio broadcasting rights, but the individuals behind the microphone continue to enjoy a status in the hearts of the Cardinals faithful that is almost comparable to the star players on the diamond.

France Laux was the first well-known announcer of Redbirds baseball, taking to the airwaves in 1929 and serving in the booth regularly until the outbreak of World War II, after which he returned to work sporadically through 1953. Throughout the 1930s, Laux was the most frequent announcer in the booth for national broadcasts of both the World Series and the All-Star Game.

Born in the city of St. Louis as Harry Carabina in 1914, Harry Caray entered his hometown broadcast booth in 1945, and over the next quarter of a century, he attained immense popularity among the city's fans as the voice of the Cardinals at KMOX radio. He was also outspoken in his opinions regarding team decisions, and following a spat with owner Gussie Busch, Caray left the Cardinals after the 1969 season.

Taking over for Caray as the main play-by-play man on the broadcasts was Jack Buck, Caray's radio mate since 1954. Buck soon usurped Caray as a St. Louis icon, establishing his own style and cementing his place as the top Redbirds broadcaster of all time. A steamy St. Louis or southern Illinois night could be conjured (perhaps even in the middle of winter) if one played a recording of Buck describing a Vince Coleman triple or a Mark McGwire home run. Buck, who also spent time as the sports director at KMOX, notably teamed with former players Joe Garagiola from 1955 to 1962 and Mike Shannon from 1972 to 2001 on the game broadcasts. Buck's son, Joe Buck, also worked alongside him on the radio during the 1990s, and the younger Buck also called Cardinals games on FSN Midwest cable broadcasts. (Harry Caray had also worked alongside his son Skip on St. Louis radio broadcasts during the 1960s.)

A veritable institution of the airwaves, Jack Buck's most powerful moment may have come at an incident in which he was not in the broadcast booth, and what would be one of his final public appearances in St. Louis. On September 17, 2001, six days after the terrorist attacks in New York, Pennsylvania, and Washington, D.C., Busch Stadium and the rest of Major League Baseball had re-opened for business. Before the Redbirds took the field that evening against the Milwaukee Brewers, World War II veteran Buck—frail from his battles with lung cancer, Parkinson's disease, and other ailments—gave an emotional address to the crowd, reciting a poem he had authored.

Buck passed away the following June 18, just four days before the passing of pitching Darryl Kile. His work helped ensure that

Harry Caray interviewing Cardinals manager Harry Walker, May 1955

Harry Caray broadcasting his final Cardinals game, October 1969

Jack Buck interviewing Albert Pujols, April 2001

Mike Shannon interviewing Tony La Russa, 2006

Jack Buck and Joe Buck in the Busch Stadium broadcast booth, Father's Day 1995

Jack Buck reciting his poem to the Busch Stadium crowd, September 17, 2001

love of the Cardinals and the love of country would endure for all time in the Midwest. Buck was widely respected by players and his broadcasting peers, and he was inducted into both the National Radio Hall of Fame and the National Baseball Hall of Fame, receiving the Ford Frick Award. Today, fans passing by the new Busch Stadium can hear some of Buck's famous calls from an audio display near his statue at the north end of the ballpark.

In 2006, after 52 seasons of Cardinals baseball, KMOX relinquished its coverage of the team to St. Louis talk-format station KTRS, a station in which the Cardinals owned a controlling interest. Simultaneously, veteran baseball announcer and St. Louis native John Rooney ushered in a new era of sounds for fans to enjoy.

Before the advent of cable and satellite services, television coverage of the Cardinals in the St. Louis area was limited to mostly away games. Local TV stations such as NBC affiliate KSDK and independent KPLR were the primary deliverers of Cardinals baseball into people's homes. Jay Randolph provided much of the television commentating as this medium grew in St. Louis as a means of regularly transmitting Cardinals baseball. Al Hrabosky, Rick Horton, and others offer the color commentary and continue the tradition of Buck, Shannon, Joe Garagiola, Gabby Street, and Dizzy Dean as notable Cardinals announcers, although Dean mostly covered Browns games while announcing in St. Louis.

Dizzy Dean (center) calling a Cardinals game, July 1943

Cardinals at spring training in Orange, Texas, 1921

Spring Training

Even though for many years St. Louis was the southernmost and western-most major league city, an escape from the late winter months of the Midwest to the warm oasis of Florida was still most welcome. The baseball tide still rises in the Sunshine State every February, and beginning in 1938, an annual escape from the cold and snow for the Cardinals and many of their fans was Al Lang Field in St. Petersburg, Florida, where the ballclub would annually ready itself for the approaching season. (The only exception during this time was during the latter portion of World War II, when the team trained in Cairo, Illinois.)

Before landing in St. Petersburg, other spring training destinations for the Redbirds included the Texas cities of Dallas (1903), Houston (1904 and 1906–08), Marlin Springs (1905), San Antonio (1918 and 1926), Hot Wells (1915–17), Brownsville, (1920), and Orange (1921–22). The team also trained in Little Rock, Arkansas (1909–1910); West Baden, Indiana (1911); Jackson, Mississippi (1912); Columbus, Georgia (1913); Stockton, California (1925); and the Florida cities of St. Augustine (1914), Bradenton (1923–24 and 1930–36), Avon Park (1927–29), and Daytona Beach (1937). In addition, the club stayed home in St. Louis for spring training in 1901, 1902, and 1919.

In 1998, the team shifted its spring operation across Florida to Jupiter on the Atlantic Coast, sharing a facility with the Montreal Expos and, later, the Florida Marlins. The 7,000-seat Roger Dean Stadium in Palm Beach County is a state-of-the-art spring ballpark, with every accommodation from skyboxes to party decks to grass-berm seating beyond the Cardinals' bullpen.

Spring training is also where Cardinals players and fans came to find the roving instruction of George Kissell, a fixture in the organization since 1940. The graduate of Ithaca College was a legend among the players, and the devout-Catholic and well-traveled Kissell has been rumored to know the mass times of every church "between St. Louis and Johnson City, Tennessee." After failing to reach the major leagues as a player, Kissell began his coaching career in the late 1940s and managed teams at several levels within the Redbirds' minor league system. He passed away in 2008.

Cardinals at spring training in St. Petersburg, Florida, 1949

Cardinals at spring training in St. Petersburg, Florida, circa 1960

Cardinals at spring training in Jupiter, Florida, 2007

St. Louis Cardinals vs. Washington Nationals, Roger Dean Stadium, March 2008

Down on the Farm

Having been credited with giving birth to the modern farm system through the efforts of Branch Rickey, the Cardinals continue their tradition of notable links to smaller communities with their minor league affiliates. The concept of a minor league system, in Rickey's mind, offered not only the chance to provide the parent club with a steady stream of prospects but also the opportunity to train those prospects in a uniform, consistent philosophy of play as espoused by the greater organization. Rickey's idea initially was financed largely with funds accrued from the sale of the Robison Field property in north St. Louis, the home ballpark that the team left in 1920 for Sportsman's Park. (The St. Louis Public School District purchased the land at the corner of Vandeventer and Natural Bridge Avenues for $250,000 in cash.)

In the early 1920s, the Cardinals had one minor league team in the organization, the Houston Buffaloes of the Texas League. The addition of the International League's Rochester Red Wings and the Keokuk Indians of the Mississippi Valley League brought the total to three in 1930. A decade later, the Cardinals farm system boasted some 31 minor league clubs, from Pocatello, Idaho, to Cooleemee, North Carolina, and from Duluth, Minnesota, to New Orleans, Louisiana. By 1960, the number of affiliates was back down to nine, and since then, the Cardinals have worked with between four and seven minor league teams at a time. The Texas League's Arkansas Travelers were the Cards' double-AA affiliate from 1966 to 2000, playing in historic Ray Winder Field.

Rickey's tradition of emphasizing player procurement from the club's minor league system continues to this day. As of 2008, the Cardinals' farm teams include the triple-A Memphis Redbirds; the double-A Springfield (Missouri) Cardinals; the single-A Palm Beach County (Florida) Cardinals, Quad Cities (Iowa) River Bandits, and Batavia (New York) Muckdogs; and the rookie-league Johnson City Cardinals in Tennessee. While the team has perpetuated long-standing relationships with places such

Dykes Potter of the Springfield Cardinals, 1931

J. D. Drew of the Arkansas Travelers, 1998

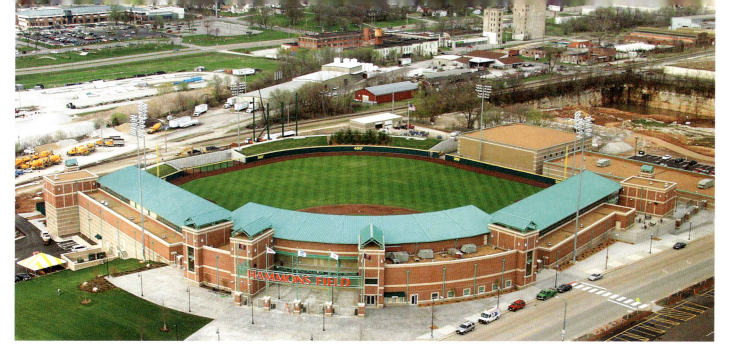

Hammons Field, home of the Springfield Cardinals, Springfield, Missouri

AutoZone Park, home of the Memphis Redbirds, Memphis, Tennessee

as Johnson City, they have also made an effort to establish minor league clubs with regional affiliations as well, evidenced by their Ozark connection of Springfield, Missouri.

After a brief stay in Springfield, Illinois (1978–1981), and even a year in the Louisiana Superdome in New Orleans (1977), the Cardinals' AAA-affiliate was housed in Louisville at Cardinal Stadium from 1982 to 1999, standing prominently along Interstate 65 on the Kentucky State Fairgrounds. After breaking the minor league attendance record in their very first Louisville season with more than 800,000 fans, the Louisville Redbirds smashed their own mark with more than a million patrons the following year. With the closure of the American Association in the late 1990s, the Cardinals found a new home for their top prospects at Tim McCarver Stadium (and later, the new AutoZone Park) in Memphis.

Bibliography and Resources

Books

Buck, Jack. *That's a Winner!* Champaign, IL: Sagamore Publishing, 1997.

Feldmann, Doug. *Dizzy and the Gas House Gang: The 1934 St. Louis Cardinals and Depression-era Baseball.* Jefferson, NC: McFarland and Company, 2000.

Feldmann, Doug. *Fleeter Than Birds: The 1985 St. Louis Cardinals and Small-Ball's Last Hurrah.* Jefferson, NC: McFarland, 2002.

Gillette, Gary, and Pete Palmer. *The ESPN Baseball Encyclopedia.* 4th ed. New York: Sterling, 2007.

Gregory, Robert. *Diz.* New York: Penguin, 1993.

Leventhal, Josh. *Baseball Yesterday & Today.* Minneapolis: Voyageur Press, 2006.

Websites

Baseball-almanac.com

Baseball-reference.com

Baseballlibrary.com

Thebaseballpage.com

Index

Al Lang Field, 136
Alexander, Grover Cleveland "Pete," 10, 85, 90, 111
Alicea, Luis, 62
Allen, Neil, 55
Alston, Tom, 36
Anaheim Angels, 67, 77
Andujar, Joaquin, 22–23, 88–89, 102–103
Ankiel, Rick, 77, 106–107
Anson, Cap, 14
Arizona Diamondbacks, 63
Arocha, Rene, 37
Atlanta Braves, 43, 53, 93, 127
AutoZone Park, 139
Averill, Earl, 130
Baltimore Orioles, 24, 28
Banks, Ernie, 28
Beazley, Johnny, 12, 16
Bell, Les, 68
Berra, Lawrence "Yogi," 98
Bilko, Steve, 53
Bordagaray, Stan "Frenchy," 108
Boston Red Sox, 13, 16–18, 20, 24, 62, 93, 98–99
Bottomley, Jim, 10, 51, 56–57, 68, 82
Boyer, Ken, 12, 18, 37, 69, 82, 112
Boyle, Jack, 44
Brazle, Al, 86, 90
Breadon, Sam, 28–29, 32, 39, 115
Brecheen, Harry "The Cat," 17, 86
Bremer, Herb, 108
Brennan, Bill, 38
Bresnahan, Roger, 44, 110
Britton, Schuyler, 28
Brock, Lou, 13, 18, 22, 32–33, 37, 74, 76, 79, 96–97, 109, 113, 118
Broglio, Ernie, 32
Brooklyn Dodgers, 8, 26–27, 44, 58, 65
Brown, Jimmy, 108
Buck, Jack, 78, 103, 132–134
Buckner, Bill, 103
Burkett, Jesse, 56, 72
Busch, August "Gussie" Jr., 28–33, 35, 116, 132
Busch Stadium, 22, 48, 74, 76, 78, 80, 97, 99, 103, 106, 109, 116, 118, 120, 122, 124, 127–128, 132, 134
Busch Stadium II, 115–118, 121, 123–124, 128
Busch Stadium III, 116–119, 121, 123, 125, 128–129
Bushong, Doc, 44, 94
Caray, Harry, 78, 132
Carleton, James "Tex," 101, 103
Carlton, Steve "Lefty," 13, 22, 87
Carpenter, Chris, 89
Caruthers, Bob, 85
Cepeda, Orlando "Cha-Cha," 13, 37, 53–54, 96, 109
Chamberlain, Elton "Icebox," 110
Chicago Cubs, 27–28, 32, 37, 44, 51, 55, 64, 67, 84, 92, 103–104, 106, 110, 127
Chicago White Sox, 13, 38, 80, 99
Chicago White Stockings, 14, 38

Cincinnati Reds, 35, 56, 72, 99, 106
Claiborne, John, 33
Clark, Jack, 22, 55, 83
Clark, Will, 35
Clayton, Royce, 67
Cleveland Indians, 130
Cobb, Ty, 56
Cochrane, Mickey, 15, 79, 101
Coleman, Vince, 76, 80–81, 96, 103, 120, 132
Collins, James "Ripper," 10, 51, 58, 82
Comiskey, Charles, 10, 14, 38, 40, 50, 72, 78
Cooper, Mort, 46, 86
Cooper, Scott, 99
Cooper, Walker, 46
Cox, Danny, 22
Crespi, Frank "Creepy," 96, 98
Crowe, George, 36
Cy Young Award, 87, 89, 92
Davis, Virgil "Spud," 44, 94–95, 104
Dayley, Ken, 93
Dean, Jay Hanna "Dizzy," 8, 10, 21, 26–27, 58, 84–86, 90, 94–95, 101, 103, 106, 130, 134–135
Dean, Paul "Daffy," 10, 27, 58, 94–95, 103
Delancey, Bill, 104, 106
Denkinger, Don, 19, 22
Deshields, Delino, 62
Detroit Tigers, 15, 18, 20–22, 65, 67, 100, 106, 131
Detroit Wolverines, 14
Devine, Vaughan "Bing," 32–33, 35, 99
DeWitt, William Jr., 31
Dickey, Bill, 16
DiMaggio, Joe, 16
Doak, Bill, 85
Donovan, Patsy, 72
Douthit, Taylor, 72, 77
Dunston, Shawon, 67
Durocher, Leo, 26, 28, 33, 44, 64–65, 67
Dyer, Eddie, 40–41, 90
Ebbetts Field, 27, 58
Eckstein, David, 20, 67
Edmonds, Jim, 76–77
Encarnacion, Juan, 37
Flood, Curt, 13, 22–23, 30–31, 36–37, 42, 74, 76–77, 79
Forsch, Bob, 88–89
Forsch, Ken, 89
Fournier, Jack, 51
Foutz, Dave, 84–85
Foxx, Jimmie, 61, 116
Franks, Herman, 45
Freehan, Bill, 22
Frisch, Frankie, 10, 21, 27, 29, 37, 39–40, 56, 58, 61, 64, 78, 84, 108, 130
Fuller, Shorty, 94
Gaetti, Gary, 71
Gant, Ron, 76
Garagiola, Joe, 46, 98, 132, 134
Gas House Gang, 10–11, 15, 26, 39, 51, 58, 64, 82, 94, 96, 100, 104, 109

Gehrig, Lou, 14
Gelbert, Charlie, 64
Gibson, Bob, 8, 12–13, 18–19, 22, 32, 36–37, 46, 86–87, 89–90, 96–97, 118, 130
Gibson, Jerry, 122
Gilkey, Bernard, 76, 98
Glaus, Troy, 71
Gleason, Bill, 64
Gold Glove Award, 48–49, 53, 55, 66–67, 69, 74, 77, 80, 87
Gonzalez, Mike, 36–37
Green, David, 74, 103
Grimes, Burleigh, 85
Groat, Dick, 37, 65
Guerrero, Pedro, 55
Hafey, Chick, 56, 72
Haines, Jesse, 10, 85, 90–91
Hallahan, Bill "Wild Bill," 85, 130
Hammons Field, 139
Hancock, Josh, 106
Hannegan, Robert, 28
Harrell, Ray, 108
Hartnett, Gabby, 27
Hays, Ernie, 109
Hemus, Solomon "Solly," 40, 96
Hendrick, George, 76, 82, 103
Hernandez, Keith, 54
Herr, Tommy, 62–63, 70
Herzog, Dorrel "Whitey," 13, 19, 22–23, 34–35, 42–43, 66, 80, 96, 103
Hoerner, Joe, 90–91
Hopp, Johnny, 52
Hornsby, Rogers, 8, 10, 14, 39, 51, 56–58, 61, 68, 82
Horton, Rick, 93, 134
Houston Astros, 89, 118, 126
Howsam, Bob, 33
Hrabosky, Al, 91–92, 134
Huggins, Miller, 38–39, 60–61
Isringhausen, Jason, 93
James, Charlie, 98
Javier, Julian, 37, 62, 79
Jocketty, Walt, 34–35
Jones, Nippy, 53
Jordan, Brian, 76, 80–81, 99
Jupiter, FL, 99, 137
Kansas City Royals, 19, 22, 25, 48, 66, 76, 92, 99, 103–104
Keane, Johnny, 33, 40–41, 43
Kennedy, Adam, 62
Kile, Darryl, 104–106, 132
King, Charles "Silver," 84, 94
Kissell, George, 136
Konetchy, Ed "Big Ed," 50
Kurowski, George "Whitey," 12, 16, 68, 96
La Russa, Tony, 13, 20, 34–35, 43, 104, 133
Lahti, Jeff, 93
Landis, Kennesaw "Mountain," 21
Lanier, Max, 41, 86
Lankford, Ray, 76, 99
Latham, Arlie, 68, 72, 78
Laux, France, 132
Lee, Derrek, 27
Lezcano, Sixto, 34
Littell, Mark, 92

Lohse, Kyle, 89
Los Angeles Dodgers, 8, 27, 67, 71, 93, 120, 126
Ludwick, Ryan, 77
Mack, Connie, 15, 39
Mantle, Mickey, 18
Marion, Marty, 40, 65, 110
Maris, Roger, 13, 18, 55, 69, 74
Marrero, Eli, 49
Martin, Johnny "Pepper," 10, 15, 68, 70, 72, 78–79, 94–95, 108, 110, 130
Matheny, Mike, 49
Maxvill, Dal, 34–35, 65, 67, 80
McBride, Arnold "Bake," 74, 76, 79
McCarthy, Tommy, 72, 78
McCarver, Tim, 12–13, 37, 46–47, 49, 131
McClellan, Kyle, 99
McDaniel, Lindy, 90
McDonald, Joe, 35
McGee, Willie, 19, 34, 74–77, 80, 108
McGinnis, George Washington "Jumbo," 94
McGraw, John, 38, 40
McGwire, Mark, 27, 35, 54–55, 82–83, 132
McKechnie, Bill, 39
Medwick, Joe "Ducky," 10, 21, 32, 44, 51–52, 58, 72, 82, 96, 100–101, 103
Miles, Aaron, 62–63
Milwaukee Braves, 62
Milwaukee Brewers, 19, 24–25, 48, 74, 104, 132
Minnesota Twins, 19, 25, 63
Mize, Johnny "Big Cat," 11, 52, 54, 58, 82, 96
Molina, Yadier, 37, 49
Montreal Expos, 89, 136
Moon, Wally, 74
Moore, Terry, 68, 72–73, 77
Mozeliak, John, 35
Mulder, Mark, 89
Mura, Steve, 34
Musial, Stan "The Man," 8, 11, 16, 30, 33, 36, 41, 52–53, 58–59, 68–70, 73–74, 82, 96–97, 108–109, 118, 131
MVP Award, 20, 44, 46, 51–54, 56, 58–59, 61, 65, 67, 69–70, 80, 84, 86–87, 98, 104, 131
Narron, Sam, 45
New York Giants, 8, 14, 26–27, 38–40, 44, 52, 56, 61–62, 82, 100
New York Mets, 43, 47, 54–55, 62, 93, 99
New York Yankees, 14–16, 18, 33–34, 36, 38, 40, 46, 52, 62, 64, 68–69, 80, 87, 90, 98–99, 130
Nichols, Charles "Kid," 96–97
Nieto, Tom, 48
Northrup, Jim, 22
O'Farrell, Bob, 39, 44
O'Neill, James "Tip," 56, 72, 82
Oakland A's, 13, 35, 55, 89
Oberkfell, Ken, 62, 70
Oquendo, Jose, 62
Orta, Jorge, 22
Ott, Mel, 82
Owen, Marv, 21
Owen, Mickey, 11, 44–45
Ownbey, Rick, 55
Padgett, Don, 45
Pagnozzi, Tom, 48–49, 70
Pena, Tony, 48
Pendleton, Terry, 70

Pesky, Johnny, 17, 62
Philadelphia Athletics (A's), 15, 39, 79, 116
Philadelphia Phillies, 31, 44, 46, 67, 71, 74, 83, 87, 89
Pittsburgh Pirates, 65, 67, 76, 90
Politte, Cliff, 99
Porter, Darrell, 48, 104, 122
Pujols, Albert, 8, 27, 37, 55, 59, 69, 82–83, 96, 113, 133
Quinn, Joe, 37
Randolph, Jay, 134
Reitz, Ken, 70
Renteria, Edgar, 37, 67
Rice, Del, 46
Rickey, Wesley "Branch," 28, 32–33, 35, 38, 44, 58, 104, 138
Rizzuto, Phil, 16
Robinson, Jackie, 122
Robinson, Kerry, 99
Robinson, Yank, 60, 94
Robison, Stanley, 28, 115
Robison Field, 114–115, 120, 138
Roger Dean Stadium, 99, 136–137
Rolen, Scott, 71
Rookie of the Year, 59, 74, 93
Rooney, John, 134
Ruffing, Red, 16
Ruth, Babe, 14, 44, 64
Sadecki, Ray, 53–54
Saigh, Fred, 28–29
Sallee, Slim, 84–85
San Diego Padres, 34, 36, 66
San Francisco Giants, 8, 49, 53, 103, 126
Sanders, Ray, 52
Schoendienst, Albert "Red," 11, 13, 30, 34, 42–43, 61–62, 69, 96–97, 118, 131
Schumaker, Skip, 77
Scott, Tony, 79
Shannon, Mike, 37, 69–70, 74, 98, 128, 132–134
Sherdel, Bill, 85
Siebert, Dick, 108
Silver Slugger Award, 66–67
Simmons, Ted, 46–48
Sisler, Dick, 53, 98, 109
Sizemore, Ted, 62
Slaughter, Enos "Country," 11–12, 17, 30, 68, 73, 96, 118
Smith, Hal, 46
Smith, Lee, 93
Smith, Lonnie, 74–76, 96, 103
Smith, Osborne "Ozzie," 8, 27, 34, 64, 66–67, 96, 118
Sosa, Sammy, 27, 55
Southworth, Billy, 24, 27, 39–41
Sportsman's Park, 14, 16, 24, 26, 28, 58, 72, 78, 103, 114–116, 120, 122, 124–128, 138
St. Louis Browns (American Association), 8, 10–11, 14, 28, 38, 50, 56, 60, 64, 68, 72, 82, 84, 94, 114
St. Louis Browns (American League), 8, 16, 24–25, 28, 38, 84, 115–116, 130, 134
St. Louis Perfectos, 8–9, 28
St. Louis Rams, 118, 120
St. Petersburg, FL, 122, 136–137
Stanky, Eddie, 30, 40
Stearns, John, 47
Stengel, Casey, 130

Street, Charles "Gabby," 29, 39–40, 96, 134
Sullivan, Thomas Jefferson "Sleeper," 94
Sutter, Bruce, 92
Sykes, Bob, 34
Taguchi, So, 37
Tatis, Fernando, 71
Templeton, Garry, 34, 66, 79
Terry, Bill, 26
Tewksbury, Bob, 89
Texas Rangers, 67
Thevenow, Tommy, 64
Tim McCarver Stadium, 139
Toporczer, George "Specs," 94
Torre, Joe, 13, 43, 53–54, 70
Triple Crown, 52, 56, 58
Tudor, John, 76, 88–89
Tyson, Mike, 62
Van Slyke, Andy, 76, 80
Veeck, Bill, 116
Viña, Fernando, 62–63
Von der Ahe, Chris, 28
Walker, Harry "The Hat," 17, 40, 113
Walker, Oscar, 82
Warneke, Lon, 108
Washington Nationals, 137
Weiland, Bob, 108
White, Bill, 36–37, 53
White, Ernie, 86
Wilks, Ted, 90
Williams, Ted, 16–17
Wills, Maury, 79
Wilson, Hack, 82
Wilson, Jimmie, 44–45
Womack, Tony, 62
World Series, 14–16, 18, 25, 27, 38, 67, 98–99, 104, 132
    1926 Series, 14, 39, 44, 64, 90
    1928 Series, 15, 39
    1930 Series, 15, 85
    1931 Series, 11, 15, 39, 45, 61, 78–79
    1934 Series, 15, 21, 51, 58, 78–79, 82, 100–101
    1942 Series, 11, 12, 16, 40, 68
    1943 Series, 11, 16, 86
    1944 Series, 11, 16, 24–25, 40
    1946 Series, 16–17, 62, 98, 126
    1964 Series, 12–13, 18, 23, 32, 36, 40–41, 46, 62, 69, 87
    1967 Series, 18–19, 43, 47, 79
    1968 Series, 18, 22, 65
    1982 Series, 13, 18, 31, 42, 48, 70, 74–76, 92, 103–104, 127
    1985 Series, 13, 19, 22–23, 25, 66–67, 93, 102
    1987 Series, 13, 19, 63
    2004 Series, 13, 20
    2006 Series, 13, 20, 31, 37, 43, 49, 106, 127
Worrell, Todd, 93
Wrigley, Phillip K., 28
Wrigley Field, 74, 104, 127
Zeile, Todd, 70

About the Author

Doug Feldmann is the author of eight books, the majority of which focus on baseball history and the sport's sociological impact on urban and small-town America. He is an associate professor in the College of Education at Northern Kentucky University and a part-time scout for the Cincinnati Reds. His previous books include *Dizzy and the Gashouse Gang: The 1934 St. Louis Cardinals and Depression-Era Baseball*; *Fleeter Than Birds: The 1985 St. Louis Cardinals and Small Ball's Last Hurrah*; and *El Birdos: The 1967 and 1968 St. Louis Cardinals*.